TAKING

C000064719

BACK

Based on a True Story

BY DENIS MURPHY

"Everything can be taken from a man but one thing; the last of the human freedoms - to choose one's attitude in any given set of circumstances, to choose one's own way."

- Viktor E. Frankl

Taking My Life Back
Based on a True Story

Published by Happy & Fun Lifestyle LLC

Copyright © 2019

Denis Murphy

All rights reserved

ABOUT THE AUTHOR

As a linguist, computer programmer and podcast host Denis is passionate about helping more people reach new levels of purpose, fulfillment and happiness.

He uses his unique insights into human psychology to help his audience understand who they are and the life they are capable of living.

Using his podcast platform which is available worldwide: "The Happy Mindset", Denis helps share the understanding that you can always dig deeper and choose to lead a happy and fulfilling life regardless of what happens to you.

He believes that it all begins with a conscious decision and a mindset shift. On his podcast, he interviews guests from around the world to uncover the real person and the real lessons behind their success.

DEDICATION

To my family who helped me through my darkest moments even when I didn't have the words to truly express the chaos playing out inside my head.

To my 22-year-old self, this book contains the lessons I learned in my 20's because out of the darkness you are about to go through you made the decision to take your life back into your own hands. I am very grateful that you made that decision.

ACKNOWLEDGEMENTS

I wish to take the opportunity to gratefully acknowledge the assistance and contribution to several individuals, without whom the completion of my book would not have been possible. First and foremost, I would like to thank Lisa Caprelli. Without Lisa's experience, guidance, and never-ending generosity, Taking My Life Back wouldn't exist.

Thank you to the creative skills and imagination of Davey Villalobos who took my written words and brought Taking My Life Back to life, I wanted to be a cartoonist as a child, so I am delighted to see your animations in my book.

Thank you to Amanda Williams, whose editorial skills and helpful directions were essential in bringing the book together.

To Claire Ashman, thanks for reading the first draft of the book, your input was greatly needed and appreciated, you sharing your story greatly helped me to share mine. To Jodie Michelle Lane, thanks for proofreading this book and for sharing your story with me.

To Micheal Hilton, thanks for setting up the Man Cave and helping me to finally own my story.

I also want to express my deepest gratitude to my family for their support, patience, and perseverance over the years.

Thank you, Mom and Dad, for always being there when I need you most and for having a room ready no matter how old I am. Thank you, Norita, Shane and Anna Maria for encouraging me and giving me advice that has helped me to follow my own unconventional path.

Finally, thank you to all my friends, mentors and podcast guests who I have had the pleasure of getting to know over the years, this book wouldn't have been possible without you all.

Thank you to each one of you.

This book deals with mental illness, if this book raises any issues for you then seek medical help from your GP or a trained psychiatrist. This was the first step that I took on my road to recovery.

This book was written with the intention of showing you the journey I went on in my 20's to transform my trauma into a positive force in my life.

It's my sincere hope that this book will help you to find your own path in life and help you to use the obstacles and challenges that life will inevitably throw your way.

By writing this book I hope to play my part in ending the stigma and normalising the conversation when it comes to talking about our mental health and well-being.

If you would like to learn more about how you can help to create the right conditions for positive conversation in Ireland then check out the wonderful work that See Change Ireland are doing: https://seechange.ie

CONTENTS

CHAPTER 1

THE WEEK FROM HELL

"The only difference between genius and insanity is that genius has its limits."

- Albert Einstein

Crossing the Line

A part of me knew I was drifting dangerously close to the edges of my sanity. As I reflect back on what happened almost a decade later there are certain key memories that have left an imprint on me to this day.

It was only beginning to really dawn on me that my thinking was becoming irrational, and I was slowly losing contact with reality when it was too late.

As my thoughts became more and more erratic and the stories more compelling, I was beginning to get a first-hand experience of the fine line that exists between sanity and insanity.

With each passing moment, I was beginning to feel the proverbial straight jacket tighten its grip around me as I struggled in vain to break free from my now out of control mind.

As I was writing out my thoughts in one of my streams of consciousness, I could clearly see that my thinking was getting more and more confused to the point that I was warning myself to stop in the third person.

This utterly freaked me out and I decided to stop but the damage had already been done, it was too late to turn back. My thoughts had already taken on a life of their own and there was no stopping the momentum now.

Messages from the Television

The first major warning sign that something had changed in my brain happened as I sat watching the movie *Oceans 11* with some of the students. It was coming towards the end of my teaching assistantship in France.

My French was at a near-native level by then and I had also begun to speak Spanish and Italian. A few months previously I had discovered language hacking and I had been training my brain to think outside the box and combine patterns in new ways.

I was inspired and very passionate about languages. I threw myself into it and for 3 solid months, I completely immersed myself in my work.

Unresolved Emotions

These months were a whirlwind of emotion as I felt anger, frustration, and passion all at the same time. I had so much passion for language hacking but it had somehow also managed to trigger a huge amount of anger and resentment I had been harboring towards the education system.

There were numerous other things that were also being triggered in me including the students who looked at me as lazy because they didn't consider mental work 'real work'. This also seemed to unearth resentments I was

3

harbouring towards people in my life who I felt had tried to define who I was in a negative way or even the individuals I discovered who had told barefaced lies about me behind my back.

Rural Isolation

At this stage, I was living in a remote part of France, and I was beginning to spend vast portions of my weekends alone. This didn't bother me as I was focused on cracking the language code and becoming a polyglot.

However, in those days my brain had a huge tendency to ruminate and dwell on the past but it never had this much time and space to ruminate before. Looking back, it was a recipe for disaster but at this time I was living in almost complete ignorance as to how my brain and my mind work.

The first subtle hallucination

As I sat watching *Oceans 11* something changed in my hearing. The shift was so subtle it's hard to find the right words to truly describe what actually changed.

One minute I was watching the movie as if it was just another movie and the next minute, I had somehow started to hear a secret code playing behind the words in the movie.

It seemed like it was always there but I had never noticed it before. The characters on screen were speaking to me in an indirect way.

My brain was beginning to interpret the movie dialogue as being directly related to my life.

Focus on the Meaning not the Words

It was very subtle, nothing had changed in the words spoken, the plot of the movie was still the same but the meaning behind the words was fundamentally different.

The movie was layered. On one level there was the movie and on another level the actors were letting me know of what was being said behind my back, and they were also letting me know of what was happening in my life now and what was going to happen in the future.

My brain was interpreting what they were saying metaphorically which meant that it didn't matter what words they specifically used, it could always be related back to my life.

It was the meaning that mattered and not the specific words. Focusing on the meaning rather than the specific words was one of the insights that enabled me to start hacking foreign languages a few months prior to this.

I didn't know what to think, it felt real, and I was aware that I was the only one noticing this. If I had tried to explain this change to someone else, they would have thought I was nuts, so I kept this first change in my perception to myself.

The Gradual Alteration of my Known World

Up until I attended a friend's birthday party signs were appearing that all was not well but I hadn't yet reached the point where I needed to send out an SOS for urgent help.

The shift in my perception of movies gradually leaked its way into other programs. I was now interpreting negative and positive world events in the newspaper and on television as happening because of me.

My interactions with other people was the next thing to be altered. Every conversation I was having or any conversation I overheard was about me, even if the words held no relevance at all, my brain interpreted them in this way.

My senses at this time were heightened and on my final weekend in my dorm room, I had convinced myself that someone was trying to break in. When nobody was there and I went back to my room, even the slightest of noises had me on edge for the rest of the night.

Alcohol – the tipping point

A drink of beer is what finally tipped me over the edge. I hadn't drunk alcohol for a couple of weeks but once I had started to sip my first beer all hell broke loose inside my head.

Up until this point my brain was highly sensitive to danger and it was interpreting everything in an egocentric manner. Although this was a difficult and confusing experience, I was able to function and get on with my day. This all changed when the voices emerged.

The Controlling Voices

At first, the whispers were sporadic. It felt like someone was whispering in my ear but as I looked around me and noticed that everyone was carrying on as normal, I started to realise that something was wrong.

The voices grew increasingly louder and more aggressive, it still felt like there was no way these voices were coming from inside my own head.

They were intrusive, judgmental and relentless. I still thought they were definitely coming from somewhere external; this didn't sound like my internal life narrator.

I don't think I was aware of the narrator inside my head back then, but I was hearing multiple voices in the same way your ears would perceive people talking and shouting at you. These voices were threatening, menacing and utterly terrifying to listen to.

As I rushed to the bathroom and the voices followed me I knew I was in serious trouble. There was no distance between the voices and my sense of self, they had completely overpowered me.

In a rational mind when a conscious thought or a bunch of conscious thoughts enter your head you intuitively know you have the freedom to accept, reject or even ignore them.

You might sometimes feel uncomfortable with the types of thoughts entering your mind, but you can generally manage to carry on and shrug it off.

Until you start believing and internalising the thoughts you know that the thoughts can't make you do anything you don't want to do, and they can't bully you.

You know thoughts are powerless without action. That part of my brain was somehow gone, and I was up shit creek without a paddle.

I walk alone...

I was at the party for a night and half of the following day. It was all a blur to me the following day as some of the people I was with quizzed me on whether I was OK and whether I had taken any drugs.

Although the night was a blur between auditory and visual hallucinations I can remember some of the thoughts and the emotions I felt. I can remember feeling terrified when the voices appeared. This was followed by confusion and feelings of being completely alone in the world. I also felt a huge amount of regret when I thought I had died.

I can remember thinking people were plotting against me. Rooms also looked different to what they first looked like when I got to the party. One person looked like the grim reaper. Conspiracy theories ran through my head, while the words of a Green Day song 'I walk alone..' echoed in my ears. I can remember calling my parents for help and speaking at one hundred miles an hour.

There were religious undertones to some of my hallucinations. The host had a pet snake which reminded me of the Garden of Eden. At one point I was the Messiah and I thought people would betray me and eventually also kill me because I knew too much about how the world works.

I would later learn from reading *Brain on Fire* by Susannah Cahalan that these sorts of thoughts and emotions can come from an overstimulation of the temporal lobes in the brain, the part which houses the hippocampus and amygdala which are responsible for emotion and memory.

A False Reality

It wasn't just my conscious thoughts that were being altered, it was my entire perception. I was trapped inside a false reality where I couldn't trust my feelings, thinking, hearing or sight – my perception of life itself.

A few days later I was on a plane home from France. As one of the teachers drove me to the airport I had hallucinations about her saying strange things, breaking speed limits and telling me the police turned a blind eye to it for the teachers at the school.

Going Home...

When I arrived home to Ireland I had become so confused by my experience that I found myself questioning where I had spent the past year.

I thought to myself that none of my family and friends had seen any of the people I was with in France. I wondered whether it was all a figment of my imagination, that perhaps the school didn't even exist and I had spent the year in the wilderness by myself.

The whole thing was a blur, at the start I was trying to make sense of it all with my thinking. I was trying to make sense of a surreal and distorted reality with the same types of thoughts that were creating it. Thankfully I eventually realised the futility behind this.

What is reality?

It's difficult to truly convey what the experience was like to someone who hasn't had a similar experience. As I have mentioned, it wasn't the experience of my conscious mind simply telling me a bunch of lies that I was innocently believing.

Rather in these moments, my perception of reality had fundamentally been altered and my brain was trying to make sense of what was happening while it was playing its part in creating this new reality.

It felt like I was in another realm, fully immersed in the madness of my unconscious mind. I didn't have any words to describe what I was experiencing and I had no idea what the future now had in store for me.

However, what I did know was that I could never unsee what I had just seen. My life was either going to go down a very dark and bleak path, or I was going to somehow manage to create an uplifting path for myself built from the lessons' chaos was intent on teaching me.

CHAPTER 2

THE LABEL

"What you resist not only persists but will grow in size." - Carl Jung

Arriving home from France

I was relieved that finally, a professional had a word that explained that what I had been experiencing over the past couple of days was in fact very real.

I had just come back from France a few days earlier. Between the visual and auditory hallucinations, I am surprised I was able to make it home in one piece.

The most frustrating part about experiencing a problem with your brain is that it plays out completely inside your own head.

At first, nobody believes you or if they do, they think you are on drugs or being overly dramatic. Nobody could comprehend just how bad it was. I mean how could they know; I didn't even know this was possible myself.

My brain had had enough and now it felt like it had turned on me. For all I knew, the Salvador Dali like reality I had somehow managed to find myself in was perhaps what the rest of my life was going to look like.

A waking nightmare

Never in my wildest dreams did I think that taking my mental health for granted could ever lead me here.

When I eventually saw a psychiatrist, his assessment shed light on the fact that my brain was in a state of psychosis.

Initially, I didn't put much thought into what this meant, I was too out of it at this stage, not knowing what to believe anymore.

I had been living with auditory and visual hallucinations for nearly a week at this point, my paranoia had been feeding me all sorts of stories, and I was completely disillusioned by everything and everyone.

Bouncing between mania and depression

On top of this, the emotions I was experiencing were a blend of mania and depression. In one moment I felt on top of the world with the clearest of minds and in the next there was a black cloud hung over me and the world was out to get me and make a fool of me.

Once I received the correct antipsychotic medication (Abilify) the hallucinations disappeared almost immediately. The extremity in my emotions also waned.

However, the memories stayed with me, and I was functioning like a zombie terrified and confused by my reality for quite some time after this.

The fear of social stigma

All of these emotions I kept locked up on the inside. I had all these doubts about my long-term mental health, at one point I was worried that I was displaying early onset signs of schizophrenia.

For a long time I kept all these emotions and thoughts to myself, I didn't want social stigma to make my situation even worse.

This was Ireland in 2010, a time before there were any conversations about mental health in the mainstream.

I was afraid if anyone knew what had happened to me then it would affect my job prospects and even my prospects of keeping and making friends.

Looking back on this time I am glad I kept my emotions and thoughts to myself. I needed someone I could trust and who could actually understand what I had been through.

An understanding not purely from a textbook point of view but from an experiential one. I wouldn't have been able to distinguish such a person with the headspace I was in at this time.

The words antipsychotic & psychotic episode

Initially, when the psychotic episode happened, I spent all my energy trying to harness my will to make myself better. Taking medication was the last thing I wanted to do.

My logic was that if I didn't take medication then this never happened, that I'm not mad and that I would never have to deal with the words psychotic episode and antipsychotic medication.

Thankfully I began to realise that the problem with crazy people is that they don't realise they're crazy. Accepting I had a problem opened up to the doors to receive help.

I wasn't supposed to drink alcohol while on medication. At that time, I couldn't imagine functioning in a social setting without a drop of alcohol.

One of the side effects of the medication was that I frequently felt lethargic and lacking in energy and I would often need to go for a nap during the day.

While taking medication was difficult for my body on a physical level it was even more challenging for me to accept on a mental and an emotional level.

The dark side of living in ignorance

I think the toughest part for me to deal with mentally was the language that was used to describe my condition.

Imagine within a matter of a week going from someone who identified as a 'normal' and functioning human being to all of a sudden needing to process and make sense of words like psychotic episode and antipsychotics.

When my mind thought of these words it immediately saw images of straight jackets, 'crazy' people, people convulsing and even electric shock treatment.

My mind had no way of separating a person from their condition when it came to mental health issues. I didn't learn about any of this at school, and I was a college graduate at this stage.

It was easy for me to see that a person is not their broken leg. If someone broke a leg, I had no frame of reference for other people referring to someone as the guy or girl who broke their leg.

However, I did have frames of reference in my mind for people who referred to other people as the person who had a breakdown or the person who is mad.

Viewing my temporary condition as myself

At that time all these words represented a reality I refused to acknowledge let alone allow myself to live in.

A reality where some people would refer to me as mad behind my back and a reality where I would live in a sedative manner to numb and ignore the pain. So, I took my medication and left this world as quickly as I entered it.

It was clear to me that in this world I was viewing myself through the lens of my condition and I would never fully recover as long as this perception remained in place.

Breaking my predefined limitations

I didn't seek counseling; I didn't look for advice and I didn't look for someone to explain my experience to me. By this stage, I had had more than enough of letting the outside world define who I was.

Don't get me wrong, I'm very grateful to the psychiatrist and the medication for bringing my brain back into balance.

I was one of the lucky ones, the first drug he prescribed me worked. But there was no human spirit here, just a diagnosis, prognosis, and drugs.

My intention was a full recovery and to see this as an opportunity to build my life on a solid foundation this time around.

Don't throw the baby out with the bathwater

At this point it's important to mention that when I was in this most helpless and vulnerable of states my initial impulse was to try and jump out of it as quickly as possible and forget it ever happened.

But in turning a blind eye to it and accepting the 'normal' way of perceiving mental illness as a skeleton to be kept firmly shut in the closet I would have lost so many invaluable lessons and insights.

These lessons have taught me more about life and human potential than 18 years of formal education.

CHAPTER 3

ROCK BOTTOM – WHERE YOUR LIFE BEGINS

"Rock bottom became the solid foundation on which I rebuilt my life." - J.K. Rowling

Moving from Rock Bottom

The future looked very dark and bleak. I felt a lot of fear, shame, and embarrassment. I felt weak, different and isolated; the easy option would have been to give up hope. But within the darkness, a few cracks of light began to emerge.

One of my first empowering thoughts was *you can use this to make you stronger if you want to look at it that way.* Followed by *if the human spirit is unconquerable, now is my time to test this for myself.* Another was; *what happened to that boy who was imaginative and loved to learn and create?*

Releasing some Stale Old Thoughts

Somewhere along the line, I had become a shadow of my former self without really noticing what was happening to me. I thought to myself that if I was that boy once, I could find a way to reconnect with him again.

In any other situation, I would have allowed my insecurities to brush these thoughts a side as quickly as they had entered my mind. For many years I had allowed my environment to draw out my cynical side but I was at rock bottom and I had had enough of my mind bullying me. I was adamant that something was going to fundamentally change for the better.

So for the first time in years, I mustered up enough courage to tell my most crippling insecure thoughts to kindly fuck off. With that, I decided to make it my mission to understand my mind and brain like I never had before.

The power of a curious mind

The "p" word combined with the power of a Google search meant that I could now conduct my own investigation and do my own research. It was my first step on my path to becoming a self-directed learner. It was a daunting and overwhelming task to undertake.

When it came to my education I had largely internalised the spoon-feeding mindset due to a lack of motivation and desire to learn.

After years of suppressing my curiosity for fear, it would lead me astray, in my rock bottom moment I had finally decided that it was time to set it free.

Psychosis and anti-fragility

I'm aware that most people don't tend to approach mental illness with a desire to learn and grow from it.

To begin with, I didn't either. Mental illness and the notion of anti-fragility don't tend to go hand in hand.

My experience with psychosis was deeply traumatising and overwhelming but I had made the firm decision that this experience was going to make me rather than break me.

This decision allowed me to relatively quickly shift my focus and attention towards problem-solving rather than to remain stuck in the problem or even move backwards. Among the first things I paid more attention too was my relationship with labels.

My relationship with labels

Growing up, I hated labels with a passion. Labels are often used as a lazy way for the archaic black and white mind to make some sort of sense of the world without having to expend time and energy on understanding life's many subtle nuances.

To give you an insight into why I started here and why I saw shifting my mindset as a viable option I will first take you back to the relationship I developed with labels and how I unintentionally created a strongly resistant mindset to them as a young boy.

Chapter 4

The Illusory Power of Words

"The pen is mightier than the sword."

- Edward Bulwer-Lytton

Hollow Words

Most people at some point have heard the phrase 'sticks and stones may break my bones but names will never hurt me'. In the schoolyard playground I often heard it but I never honestly believed the hollow words I was met with to be true.

As a child, teenager and well into my adult years I believed that words had the power to define who I am in both a positive and a negative way.

Still to this day, the deceptive nature of a word catches me out. Why does it matter to me what my job title sounds like to other people? Why does a word that draws attention to a 'flaw' in my personality or physical appearance cut so deep?

My relationship with the word foreigner

As a child I didn't look Irish, I still don't for that matter, but Ireland in the 1990's was a different place in a different time, and I was a pretty insecure kid.

At the time there weren't many foreign national people. It wouldn't be until the early 2000's that we had the first wave of immigration as Poland joined the European Union.

In 1990's Ireland I stood out for how I looked. I had dark hair, brown squinty eyes, and a sallow complexion pretty much all year round.

25

Basically, I was the exact opposite of the stereotypical pale, blue-eyed, red-haired, freckled kid.

I often heard labels like 'foreigner' or 'Chinese' used to describe me. More often than not these terms were used with the intention of belittling me. This led to me developing an unhealthy complex with these words and what they represented.

You don't belong here

Like any human being, I arrived here on this earth with the primal need to feel like I belong. However, it was difficult to believe I belonged when the country I was growing up in was subtly sending me the message that I might belong somewhere but not here.

I was a child at the time, so I wasn't able to articulate why I was feeling such anger and rage boil up inside me when I was met with people who felt entitled to label me in this way.

I couldn't verbalise the anger and rage in a healthy way so I had no other option but to swallow and suppress it.

Even as a child I thought it was silly and trivial of me to focus on these things but my mind had other ideas.

My biggest psychological dysfunction at the time manifested in my need to fit in as much as possible.

My country was subtly telling me that I didn't belong here from a very young age, so I was going to do as much as possible to prove it wrong.

My relationship with the word swat

Around the age of 10, a new label started to creep into my life in the form of the "swat" label, meaning "geek". Again, this word managed to crawl under my skin and poke at my need to fit in.

I tried my best to adjust my actions and behaviours to avoid this label sticking. Over time this decision manifested in the form of me losing interest in education and school and my grades gradually becoming average.

Fixed Mindset Culture

In my mind, if you wanted to fit in then average was the best place to be. To be fair the education system itself wasn't exactly inspiring me to want to learn in the first place.

It wasn't that I had bad teachers, some were good and some weren't, but the main thing that turned me off education was this fixed mindset culture that seemed to permeate through it.

I started to get a sense of the fixed mindset culture in my early teens when I began to wonder what was the point of school when my peers seemed to value someone who could get good grades without any effort.

Someone who put in lots of hours studying to get a good grade was deemed a 'swat', someone who put in work and still got a bad grade was 'not bright', someone who didn't study and got bad grades was somehow 'cool' for not caring, while someone who didn't seem to put in much study and got good grades was deemed some sort of 'natural genius'.

This belief that natural talent should be valued and effort undervalued only serves to undermine the purpose of education and leads to a toxic fixed mindset and a negative relationship with learning. I had this mindset in abundance.

Link Between Physical & Psychological Pain

Around the age of 16 or 17, feeling foreign and different became less of an issue for me. I was a teenager who now had acne to deal with. Instead of feeling foreign or being a "swat", acne now became the thing that I felt embarrassed and insecure about.

The more I focused on it being a problem for me, the more it seemed to get worse, to the point where I needed antibiotics for the cysts that I developed from picking and obsessing about them.

My experience with acne was the first time I began to see the link between physical and psychological pain and it was my first glimpse into the principle that whatever you resist will persist and even magnify.

At the time I was aware that the human tendency to focus on the negatives was much easier but somewhere in the back of my mind I had this thought that maybe focusing on the positives for a sustained period of time would be worth the effort.

My negatively conditioned mind was far too strong at this point to really take the time to expand on this thought any further.

I wasn't aware of the healing properties that a silent mind could bring, I would have rathered drive myself to distraction than to sit in silence with my thoughts.

Life happens for you – if you allow it

Which brings us back to where my story begins. At the age of 22, my relationship with labels came to a head and I could no longer deny that there were serious issues that needed resolving.

It took the chemicals in my brain being out of whack for me to stop and take a closer look at my psychology.

Looking back, I can see that there were a multitude of things that happened in parallel in my final few months in France that eventually culminated in my brain's psychosis.

An obsessive focus on my work, isolation, dehydration, interrupted sleep, weight loss and an overall lack of emotional intelligence were some of the main things that stand out to me.

However, I am a firm believer that life happens for me and not to me and there is always a root cause hidden somewhere.

Therefore, I chose to use this experience as a learning experience and that simple decision is where the lessons in this book come from.

Chapter 5

Discovering My Self Talk

"The people who are crazy enough to think they can change the world, are the ones who do."

- Steve Jobs

Aren't Most People Normal?

Only 'crazy' people hear voices in their head. I had always taken this to be true and by implication, I believed that 'normal' people never heard voices in their head.

My assumption was that the majority of people were 'normal' and only a tiny fraction of people were 'crazy'.

I believed this because this is how the world appeared to me. I never had a real reason to dig any deeper, so I believed what I could see only with my eyes.

I hadn't yet heard of the Steve Jobs quote about crazy people. My image of crazy was bleak and as far removed from being pleasant as you could get. When I thought of crazy, I thought about a crazy cat lady or some weird hermit.

The life and soul of the party, the 'naturally gifted' and 'beautiful' people and the great people of this world were the exact opposite of these archetypes in my mind.

An uncomfortable set of questions

Initially, I felt like a deer caught in the headlights when I realised the voices were coming from inside my head. I couldn't wrap my head around what this meant for me.

Was I now destined for the 'loony bin'? Would I become a zombie medicated up to his eyeballs in order to function in a normal way? Would I now become a burden to my friends and family? What friends would I even have? Would people look at me differently from this point onwards? More importantly, would I look at myself differently?

These were the types of questions whizzing around inside my head at lightning speed accompanied by feelings of embarrassment, fear, confusion, and isolation. The more I entertained and analysed these questions the worse I felt.

I had aspired to do well in life, be likable, be successful and have a nice experience of life but then out of the blue life dealt me a new hand and presented me with a new reality.

I couldn't lie to myself and I wasn't foolish enough to believe that I could just sweep this experience under the carpet.

As appealing as it was to play the role of the Great Pretender, pretending everything was OK for the rest of my life didn't sit well with me.

Slowing Down

When faced with extreme levels of uncertainty I took the decision to slow down. By slowing down I am referring to mental activity rather than physical activity.

My mind had become so revved up in analysing and looking for meaning in circumstances and in other people's behaviours that it was a novelty for me to think that I could break this habit.

I didn't even know it at the time that it was a habit. I was like the Titanic who had suddenly been given a second chance to readjust my course, slow down and man the crow's nest this time.

The First Few Questions & Assumptions

The act of slowing down mentally and not believing almost every thought that entered my head started to create spaces where none previously existed.

These spaces were minimal at first, perhaps a few milliseconds between unconscious thoughts that up until then I was completely trapped inside.

In these spaces, I started to see some of the questions and assumptions behind my automatic reactions.

I was beginning to see that it wasn't the event or the person that was directly affecting how I felt. Instead, it was my relationship to it and my relationship to it was governed by how I thought about it.

Dreading the thought of something

Have you ever dreaded the thought of giving a presentation to a class, speaking to new people or speaking a new language?

I have and continue to have all these experiences. However, up until my early 20's I hadn't given serious consideration as to why I felt so controlled by these situations. Why do some people barely survive in these situations while others seem to thrive?

I guess the answer was contained in the words 'dreaded the thought'. There was a time when I would have explained these anomalies away by saying there are some people who are just naturally charismatic or that some people are more confident because they are better looking.

But seeing the change in myself and some of the people I have surrounded myself with over the last few years, I know that this isn't true.

When I started to really slow down, through my intentions along with some meditation, I started to see that my questions and my assumptions contained the answers I was looking for.

The Unconscious Monkey Mind

When I was living unconsciously to the little voice inside my head my questions were never empowering when I was in these situations and felt nervous and anxious.

The types of questions and assumptions underpinning these nervous and anxious feelings were often thoughts like *am I doing OK?, they know I don't know that much, what if I make a fool of myself?, I don't want everyone talking about me behind my back.*

All of these questions were negative and self-centered. It's little wonder why I would be feeling self-conscious, anxious and uptight with these questions whizzing around inside my head.

As I began to notice the connection between my feelings and the quality of my questions, I started to wonder *what would happen if I changed the questions?*

I had nothing to lose, I knew I didn't want to stay in that black hole of questioning that I had found myself in after my experience with psychosis.

Shift to Growth Mindset

So, I came up with my hypothesis. If my trail of thought begins with my question and my question determines what I focus on then *what if I changed the question to something more empowering? Would I start feeling more optimistic and start making better progress in my life?*

This started small but over time as I began to consciously ask myself better questions, I became less reactive and less self-conscious.

As things began to shift and change, I generally started to feel better about myself, I could focus better and I was more willing to experiment and try new things.

When something didn't go to plan, after I got over my initial disappointment, I would find myself more frequently asking w*hat can I learn from this?*

When I felt nervous or self-conscious in a situation I interrogated myself less and less with questions like *why do I have to be nervous in this situation?, how can I change this?, what is wrong with me?*

Instead I started to flip this and ask questions like *what is wrong with feeling nervous?, why do I judge myself and resist this feeling?, what if my body is intelligent and it is working for me at all times?, what is my body trying to tell me through these feelings?*

Different input, different output

As I asked myself a different set of questions and focused in a new direction my actions and behaviours also gradually started to change.

I started to write and blog online and I started to develop the habit of reading and talking about and implementing ideas.

Even though the majority of my ideas didn't go anywhere or create much of an impact I was gradually shifting my focus and my relationship with failure and this was huge for me.

With these new questions, I was more willing to face uncertainty, try new things out and generally have a better experience of life.

I was no longer dreading the automatic lines of questioning that had me feeling deflated for days on end after a perceived setback.

A real sense of hope

I began to realize that my feelings had very little to do with the situation I was faced with and everything to do with the questions and types of thoughts I was having about the situation.

Now there was real hope. You can't always change the situation you're in and you certainly can't change another person but you can always make the decision to find and change the question that is at the root of your self-talk and what you focus on.

CHAPTER 6

IMAGINATION - IT ISN'T OPTIONAL

"Knowledge will take you from A to B. Imagination will take you everywhere."

— Albert Einstein

Hiding my Imagination

As a child, I had a vivid imagination that I hadn't yet learned to be ashamed of. I was fascinated by cartoons and drawings. I loved to imagine myself living in these animated worlds where anything seemed possible.

This was in stark contrast to the 'real' world with its many imposed limitations and rules. I drew quite a lot, mainly animals and cartoon characters. I sometimes hung my drawings on my bedroom wall.

I grew up watching Don Conroy, a cartoon artist on children's television. I was mesmerized at how well he drew and I remember wanting to become a cartoonist when I grew up.

Being told that wasn't a viable career path for me was the first time I remember internalising the false belief that other people will forever determine what I can and cannot do with my life.

Forgetting my artistic nature

As I grew older the shame began to set in around my artistic side. Nobody seemed to take art or writing all that seriously.

As the years passed by, I became more and more disinterested with anything that was of an artistic nature. I wasn't interested in getting better at art or writing because it didn't seem to have value or serve a practical purpose in the world I grew up in.

I was more interested in playing football, so I let this interest take over. I enjoyed playing football and it also seemed to earn me a certain amount of respect among my peers.

I felt art and writing would only leave me open to teasing, so they took a backseat.

Language as my Creative Outlet

As a teenager language became my only creative outlet as I tentatively chose to study French at university. At the time, even something as simple as choosing to combine French with my Business degree somehow managed to make me feel uneasy.

My self-talk was frequently self-conscious back then and I felt like I needed to justify this decision to the people who wouldn't understand why choosing to study French made any practical sense.

There is always going to be someone who thinks one of your choices doesn't make sense but I wasn't aware of this at the time.

As I sat in my French classes I sometimes wondered why I was there. I cared more about the opinions of others than I did of the opinion of myself. At that time, if you had said that to me, I would have blatantly denied it.

Paranoia - my imagination in disguise

When I went through my experience with psychosis I went in and out of periods of crippling paranoia. The paranoia was insidious because it felt like I was all of a sudden discovering absolute truths that I had been ignoring my whole life.

Imagine you are Indiana Jones discovering hidden treasures at the end of some extremely dark and dangerous tunnels.

There were many moments of *ah that makes sense now*, and *how did I miss that?* I had never had this type of experience before, so I found myself trying to make sense of what was happening to me and getting utterly confused in the process.

The paranoia appeared real and justifiable to me, it didn't feel like a figment of my imagination, it felt like this was the truth of the matter and it was other people who weren't seeing things clearly.

At the time I didn't know how powerful my imagination could be. I had naively believed that I had left it behind a long time ago as I matured into a 'responsible adult'.

I had associated imagination only as a tool talented artists could take out on call to create a work of art, but I was discovering that our imagination and our capacity to tell compelling stories is innately part of who we are as human beings regardless of whether we choose to recognise this or not.

Wonky Jenga Block

What made it tricky to break out of the paranoia was that there was often a lesson hidden beneath the chaos.

The many times I betrayed my gut feeling around certain individuals and certain decisions I made in my life that didn't align with who I was at my core.

It felt like all these seemingly small and insignificant decisions were finally coming back to haunt me.

Looking back on it now I can see that the wonky jenga block at the foundation of my tower of stories was a self-image I had somehow constructed in my mind that was largely fed by what I thought other people thought of me.

It sounds very meta in hindsight but at the time this way of looking at the world was so ingrained in me; I didn't know there was another way to live.

'Normal' is a Relational Word

All throughout my teenage years and well into my early adult years I had believed that I had chosen to 'grow up' and disown my imagination.

I believed that I wasn't really that creative and I wasn't someone with their head in the clouds. At least that is what I thought I should think about myself.

I thought I was fitting in, thinking rationally about the world around me and generally being 'normal'. It's funny how I wanted to be 'normal' for such a long time without ever asking some fundamental questions like *what does 'normal' actually mean? Normal in relation to whom?*

When you start asking these questions you begin to realise that the word normal doesn't exist in a vacuum. Rather, the word normal only has a specific meaning in the world you live in. Therefore, the only person with the power to define normal for you is you.

It's questions and realisations like these that have allowed me to keep following my own path in the face of words like 'not normal' or 'weird' that crop up in my own internal self-talk when I entertain the idea of venturing well off the beaten path.

The Gift my Paranoia Gave Me

It took experiencing extreme paranoia for me to realise that having an imagination isn't optional. The key lesson I learned from my paranoia was that my largely untapped imagination had built my self-image around what I thought other people thought of me.

My paranoia wouldn't have existed if my imagination hadn't managed to create a self-image that was built on things completely outside of my control.

Although it was a torturous experience, the most confusing time of my life and I never wish to go through it again, my experience with psychosis was also a gift because it woke me up to my untapped creativity and imagination and gave me the option to consciously use them instead of unconsciously letting them continue to use me.

There is a saying when it comes to skills development that you either *use it or lose it*. When it comes to creativity and imagination my mantra is *'you either use it or it uses you.'*

Reconnecting with my Imagination in the Digital Age

Finding outlets for my creativity and imagination has done wonders for my mental health and my sense of belonging.

Until I began to write, code and speak on my podcast, I felt like a pressure cooker, slowly boiling over with anger and resentment towards a world I didn't understand and that I didn't think took the time to really understand me.

Today, I have made a conscious effort to focus my creative energy on writing and building things for myself and my audience. Learning to code has helped hone my creative skills in a digital age. It also helps me to focus my mind, think more logically and tackle one problem at a time. I enjoy building something from nothing, learning from trial and error and seeing something I created grow and evolve. It has allowed me to become less afraid of failure and to care less about what other people think of me.

Creating a podcast has given me an outlet for the deeper and more meaningful conversations that I have longed for since childhood. In a world where very, few people seem to listen to each other, writing, coding and podcasting are the tools that I use to express my creative powers and my real voice.

Believe it, see it, become it

In choosing to focus my attention on more of the things I want to be doing, I have grown to believe in the idea that *'you can't be what you can't see'*.

I never thought it was possible that I would create a podcast or write this book but it all came from a shift in how I used my imagination and what I believed was possible for me, which in turn altered my environment over time.

It has become easier to create and develop my skills with so many people in my online and offline networks doing similar things.

As human beings, we are highly adaptive creatures and while we may not have much of a choice in the environment we are born into we have a choice to tap into and harness our imagination to directly influence our environment in a positive way as we mature into adults.

CHAPTER 7

WHAT YOU FOCUS ON EXPANDS

"At the end of your little feelings there might be nothing but at the end of every principle is a promise." - Eric Thomas

Processing what had happened

In the initial months, I tried really hard to make sense of why my brain snapped but the more I tried to work things out in my head the more confused I got. I was seeking validation that this is normal and many other people go through it and come out the other side.

My biggest fear was that this was the real me and there was something wrong with me. That I was broken inside and unstable. I didn't want to think that I was inferior to others, would become dependent on them and at my core, I was mentally ill. This is not where I wanted to focus my time and energy.

My mind was so busy judging, comparing and analyzing my situation. I noticed that as this way of looking at the world continued, I was feeling worse and worse. I knew I had to break free of this pattern but I didn't know how.

With no other obvious alternatives, I did the most sensible thing and gave up. I didn't know where to focus my energy, so I checked out mentally as I thought *to hell with all of this.*

Ironically this was the first step on my path to freedom. I had assumed that I had just waved the white flag and the stubborn side of me had finally admitted defeat. But this wasn't a defeat, it was a lesson in acceptance.

The Healing Power of Acceptance

My acceptance came from the fact that I had just given up completely on analyzing the world and my relationship to it. I had stopped tapping my proverbial hammer on the screw in front of me as I realised that if I continued along these lines I may have literally screwed my life up.

To be honest, it didn't feel good at the time. It felt like I had given in to the people who champion the idea of living in ignorance as the best way to live a happy life. But I was drained and fed up and I wanted a break from my unruly mind.

It wasn't the first time I was humbled and it certainly wouldn't be the last. Being humbled by an event or another person isn't always an easy thing to process. When someone delivers your lesson in the form of a verbal attack it almost feels like they have punched you in the face and you can't hit them back.

I had this experience on a number of occasions in my teenage and early adult years and I didn't like it one bit. These experiences made me risk-averse and less inclined to voice my honest thoughts and opinions around other people.

Living with this mindset I didn't realise that it was possible to receive open and honest feedback from other people in a non-judgmental way that was meant to serve me.

The world of coaching opened my eyes to an aspect of human behaviour that was largely hidden from my view.

A treasure chest without a key

Once I had admitted defeat and learned the lesson in acceptance the space and freedom my mind needed to start healing and growing from the experience began to gradually emerge.

With this sense of new-found clarity and perspective I knew that I couldn't go back to being my old self again. It would have been like stumbling across a treasure chest and refusing to acknowledge it existed simply because I didn't yet have the key to open it.

At this point in my journey I could only sense that there was a path forward for me. I had no words, no understanding and I didn't quite know what my next steps would be but in the midst of this I found myself getting curious.

Thinking in Opposites

Quite a few of the lessons I learned came as a result of thinking in the exact opposite way to a pattern of thinking I had already internalized. I noticed that whenever I really resisted something, I tended to get more of it.

This happened when I developed a fixation with my acne, it happened when I hated when people called me 'foreign' or 'shy' and it happened when I didn't want to admit that I had lost control of my mind.

So, I had the thought *if I'm getting more of what I don't want by resisting it then why don't I just focus on what I do want instead?*

The Subconscious Mind

To do this more effectively I started reading books about the subconscious mind like *The Power of Your Subconscious Mind* by Dr Joseph Murphy.

I learned that the subconscious mind ignores the negative entirely. When you keep saying to yourself something like *I don't want to get drunk tonight and face a hangover tomorrow* all your subconscious mind picks up on is *I want to get drunk tonight and face a hangover tomorrow.*

It sounded silly to me at first but I have had this type of experience happen to me far too many times in the past to ignore the possibility that there is something to this.

When I started to think in these terms, I started to remember some of the ways I had positively been using this principle. In language learning, I noticed that whenever I took the time to learn a new word, I would tend to notice it again within a couple of days.

This helped to reinforce my learning without any real conscious effort on my part. It was as if the word had always been there somewhere in the background, but because it wasn't in my awareness, I never picked up on the frequency.

As I took an interest in brain science, I would later learn that the RAS (Reticular Activating System) was the part of the brain responsible for this.

Despite my new-found conscious application of the principle of focus, it wasn't all uphill from there. In fact, to the naked eye, things would have appeared to be sliding even further downhill for me before I began my Masters.

Further Downhill

Not long after going through psychosis, I developed pilonidal sinus, another rather embarrassing ailment. An ingrown hair on the tailbone might sound insignificant and even laughable but it required surgery and it took 3 years to recover fully from this.

Again, my embarrassment meant that I bottled this up and told nobody about it unless there was no getting around it. During this time, I frequently experienced moments of frustration where I felt like I was never going to fully heal from any of this.

Looking back, I think a good 80% of my default thoughts for the year after my week of psychosis were negative and confusing.

You're wired for survival not happiness

The brain and the mind can be unbelievably negative when we live our lives in a largely unconscious manner.

According to Jonathan Haidt, author of *The Happiness Hypothesis*, your brain is wired to help you survive, not to make you happy.

It wasn't surprising I was frequently feeling negative about myself because I still held this belief in my heart that my environment fully determined my feeling state and, in my mind, my environment couldn't have looked any bleaker.

June 2011 until July 2012 was the toughest year for me mentally, physically, emotionally and spiritually. The psychosis happened in June 2011; I started a Masters in DCU that September but it proved to be far too soon after what had happened.

The side effects from the medication I was on meant that my brain was often foggy, and I was constantly feeling tired. I had to drop out of the course after the first semester.

This was the first time I had to quit something that mattered to me. The following year I developed the pilonidal sinus, and I was also receiving unemployment assistance for a couple of months. I was frequently feeling worthless and lethargic.

Turning a Corner

It wasn't until July 2012, when I started teaching English to French teenagers in a summer camp in England, that I began to turn a corner.

I went to take a second attempt at my Masters that September, this time in Swansea, Wales. I looked at it as my shot at redemption.

It was there I met Elçin - my first psychologist friend. At the time I needed a friend. My experience with psychosis had opened my eyes to the fact that a lot of the people I thought of as friends in my life were simply acquaintances at best.

In my heart, I always knew that when it came down to it, they didn't really know or want to know who I was and I had no idea who they were either.

This realisation has ultimately given me the permission to be me and create my own path in life but it was an extremely painful realisation that took me many years to come to terms with.

I didn't think much about it at the time but during my Masters year a lot of the people I knew happened to be studying psychology.

The Mind as a Muscle

It took a lot of conscious awareness, effort, and discipline for me not to become the bitch of my own brain.

Although it was much easier to focus on the negatives and play the role of a victim, deep down I knew that this was not the life I wanted for myself. What got me through the most difficult moments was my relentless faith in principles.

I made the decision to pay attention to whatever thoughts I had that were positive and uplifting. Thoughts such as *many other people have it much worse off than I do right now* and *things can only really go up from here.*

I started training my mind to focus on what I wanted it to focus on and to block out the white noise. My reasoning was that the mind is a muscle, I hadn't been training it, which led to atrophy.

My mind's atrophy meant that I was often reacting to life. My friend's circle, the media, and society at large were all things that I was frequently triggered by.

When I didn't have the understanding to know I was being triggered I felt like I had no other option but to adapt to my environment and settle even when I often felt disconnected from it and utterly confused by it.

I didn't want to spend my life blaming society and other people for my problems, I was committed to finding solutions to them instead.

CHAPTER 8

THE POSITIVE SIDE OF DELUSIONS

*"For me, it is far better to grasp the Universe
as it really is than to persist in delusion,
however satisfying or reassuring."* - Carl Sagan

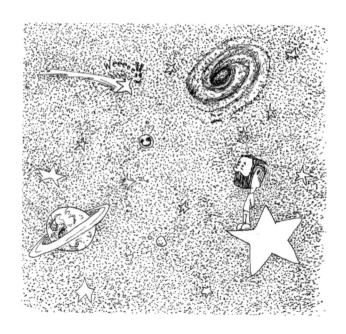

My fascination with human behaviour

Even though I never formally studied psychology, I have always been fascinated by human behaviour. When I was a teenager, I would often find myself watching war documentaries and trying to understand the sheer insanity that drove people to commit such barbaric acts upon each other.

I was equally as fascinated by the beauty that war seemingly managed to create in the form of unbreakable bonds between human beings. Incredible innovations also appeared to emerge from the necessity that war imposes upon humanity.

In World War II I found the power of propaganda utterly confusing yet also strangely intriguing. This sense of intrigue led me to think that if I ever wanted to gain a better understanding of other people than I had to begin by understanding myself better.

My relationship with the word psychology

As long as I didn't understand my own psychology, I would continue to be left wide open to being manipulated by nefarious systems and people.

I would learn that It was only after World War II that psychology shifted its focus to treating abnormal behaviour and mental illness largely because of economic reasons.

In the article *Positive Psychology An Introduction* it went on the say that in 1946 the Veterans Administration was founded and thousands of psychologists discovered that they could make a living from treating mental illness.

In 1947 the National Institute of Mental Health was founded, and academics discovered that they could get grants if their research was about pathology.

Positive psychology and high performance

I was surprised by this at first. I didn't know that psychology was ever used in a positive way. The psychology I was vaguely familiar with was of the post 1946 kind. My mental image of psychology was of a tool that was used to keep deeply troubled people under control.

With this mental image, it wasn't surprising that I wanted my brain to heal without ever stepping foot inside the office of a trained psychiatrist. This little insight into the wide-ranging world of psychology opened my mind to the world of positive psychology and high performance.

Instead of focusing on a bleak future and perceiving myself as mentally unstable and having 'demons' to live with for the rest of my life I could now channel my energy and focus on something much more positive and uplifting for my future self.

The purpose of delusions

It had never occurred to me that it was possible to observe myself and become more conscious of my own actions and behaviours.

It's so much easier to observe and judge other people but my mindset was about to start shifting as I began my informal study of psychosis.

I immersed myself in reading about psychosis and mental illness. I was so consumed about understanding what caused mental illness that I found myself spending 3 months translating a 6,000-word article called *The Healing Properties of Delusions in Schizophrenia* by Sigmund Freud from French into English for my Translation Masters.

I learned a key lesson that summer, that was pivotal in shifting my perception of the purpose of delusions and hallucinations.

Up until I researched this topic, I didn't see any purpose to delusions other than to torment their victims. But my research had managed to shed some light on the fact that learning the lessons from my delusions could heal the underlying issue and transform my mind in the process.

I started to perceive the delusions I had experienced during psychosis as a window into the madness of my unconscious mind. Within my delusions, some of my unconscious fears were presented to me, this represented a great opportunity for learning.

Heal Your World from the Inside Out

In the same way that you can't be what you can't see, I believe that you can't heal from something you can't first see exists within yourself. When I started asking better questions of myself, I noticed that some of my delusions were anchored in external illusions.

I started to ask questions that cut to the core of why I really wanted something, no matter how embarrassing it was to admit to myself. If you don't cut to the core beyond the stories that sound rational to your mind then you won't make meaningful progress.

One of my specific delusions was centered around becoming a successful online entrepreneur, who spoke multiple languages and traveled the world carefree.

The image itself wasn't the issue. I believe that the desire to grow and become the best possible version of yourself is a fundamental part of being human and a delusion bounded in rational thought often becomes the blueprint for a life well-lived.

However, flawed expectations have the power to quickly transform a vision into a toxic delusion and I had many flawed expectations.

At that time my most insidiously flawed and toxic expectation was that people would like and accept me more if I only became this unrealistic image of my successful self.

The Artist Delusion

The lessons in my delusions were multifaceted. When I acknowledged them and invited them to become my teacher instead of tormenter I began to see where I had gotten lost and wandered off my path.

During the initial stages of my experience with psychosis I had an overwhelming sense that I was put here on this Earth to be an artist.

I can distinctly remember artists suddenly representing angels on earth whose job is to help people wake up to who they are and why they are here.

This feeling came out of nowhere, I had never felt anything like it and I was convinced that this was the reality I was living in now.

I found myself believing and proclaiming that I was an artist as I became immersed in my writing.

I felt myself embodying what I was saying and like I had access to a higher power. I was suddenly beginning to get insights into why an artist would go mad from feeling like they were misunderstood by the world and being misrepresented by people who were utterly lost themselves.

In this realm the idea of someone cutting off their own ear from looking at the sheer blindness and stupidity of humanity didn't seem so mad at all.

Art was no longer constrained to paintings on a wall. I began to see art in nature, sport, fashion and anything that resembled a creative energy. Where once it was compartmentalised in my mind's eye, art now began to blend in with life itself.

As you can imagine when the medication kicked in and the delusion popped I felt deeply embarrassed and ashamed that my mind went to this place.

I wanted to forget about it and I had a strong urge to shut the door on art and creativity for the rest of my life. I didn't ever want to take the chance of going to this dark place in my mind ever again.

Initially I did shut that part down with all the energy I had left. Thankfully when I went to Swansea and started reading some of Sigmund Freud's work my mind opened to the possibility that I could somehow learn from the delusions I was immersed in when I entered this realm.

As I did this I remembered one of the questions I asked myself during the eye of the storm –

what happened to that boy who loved to learn and create?

A year later I started to write my first blog. What I have learned in this time is that your art has to mean everything to you and nothing to you all at the same time.

It's how you can learn to trust your capacity to create from your heart whilst also remaining sane and grounded in the world.

Fear Mental Imprisonment Not Stupidity

When you see the flawed expectation at the root of your delusion it's important to take the time to acknowledge to yourself on an emotional level that it's true.

Many of my flawed expectations have been rather embarrassing to admit to myself. A few years ago, I would have never admitted the root of any of my delusions in public for fear that other people would think I am weak and quite frankly an idiot.

But if you don't accept them the pattern built on top of these flawed expectations will continue to imprison you and run your life. Keep in mind that the logic that created some of these expectations were most likely created by the brain of a child who was trying to make sense of the world and their relationship to it. Have compassion for that child so you can let go of your past.

Unconscious Habits

While the antipsychotic medication meant that my delusions and hallucinations had long since disappeared, I wasn't fully satisfied with this.

I wanted to learn more about how my mind works so that I would never have to endure this form of psychological suffering again and in doing so help other people become aware of and avoid this experience altogether.

So, as I had started to shift my self-talk and what I focused on by asking better questions I was now beginning to see how much of my behaviour was simply habitual.

CHAPTER 9

CHANGING HABITS

"As the physically weak man can make himself strong by careful and patient training, so the man of weak thoughts can make them strong in right thinking." - James Allen

Is our Education System a Scam?

My first jobs after my Master's degree were customer support roles. I was grateful because these roles allowed me to use my French but I also thought to myself *couldn't I have landed these jobs without spending 5 years of my life at university?*

Initially, this question brought up a lot of negative emotions. I felt like I had been somehow conned by the education system and I wondered why it didn't occur to me to really think about what I wanted to do with my life. *Was my education not supposed to help with all this? Did I really need a degree or a Masters after all?*

After noticing that these questions and lines of logic felt toxic to me I realised that I no longer wanted to dwell on them. So, I decided to change the questions and in doing so I chose to get curious about the real world and how it actually worked.

Flicking a Switch in my Brain

I had spent so long inside an academic bubble that fundamentally disinterested me that I had lost my genuine curiosity about the world around me.

Now that I was finally living in the real world, I felt like I did when I first stumbled across language hacking, that feeling that my brain had finally switched on after years of hibernation.

69

Back in 2014 I still had a lot to learn about the brain and the mind, but I was becoming increasingly aware of the power of habit. I didn't really understand habits but I knew they had something to do with success.

I used my body as a gateway to understanding my mind, so in January 2013 I decided to develop the habit of going to the gym. I thought that if I was in physically better shape then I would also be able to think more clearly and get in better mental shape.

Starting with Physical Fitness

Around the beginning of 2014 I had put on noticeable weight, I wasn't at the point of an intervention, but I was about 13 lbs more than my usual weight.

There were probably a multitude of factors for this but the medication I was on and the recovery from pilonidal sinus would not have helped.

My intention at this time was to condition myself to enjoy going to the gym regularly. Around this time, I had the thought 'well I conditioned myself to 'enjoy' getting drunk every weekend, so I can condition myself to enjoy going to the gym.

Gamification as a Learning Tool

Through learning French, I realised that gamification was a great way to motivate me to take initial action.

When I received my worst grade in French in the first semester of my first year, I found a language lab on campus where there was software that turned learning French into a game for me.

It was nothing near the standards of today's language learning apps but I spent a lot of time in there and I went from a C student to an A student within a single semester.

The simple game this time was to decrease my body fat. The goal of measuring and seeing my body fat decrease through hard work, consistency and effort was the internal motivation I needed. Over time, I began to believe in the idea of a healthy body equals a healthy mind.

Face Your Fears One Day at a Time

Once I began to train myself physically it wasn't long before I had the desire to train myself mentally. Through discovering the power of my questions, I was able to gradually start shifting my self-talk but I knew there was much more power I had yet to tap into.

I had never consciously trained my mind before, so I didn't really know where to begin or even what to expect. I was actually very afraid of my mind at this point because I was still living with the memories of how badly things can go wrong with the mind.

But I knew something had to change, so I gradually overrode this fear by taking small consistent daily actions steps. I simply chose to start with what I had and work from there.

Thankfully I didn't have to create this path based on blind faith alone. Books and people eventually became my guides. They helped to instill the belief in me that there is much more to a human being than meets the eye.

The James Allen quote from *As A Man Thinketh*, at the beginning of this chapter, gave me the faith that it was possible to train my mind to think better.

Brutal Self-Honesty

It may sound harsh that I considered myself a man of weak thought at this time. At this stage, I had a Master's degree and I had lived through my experience with psychosis without it fully breaking my mind and spirit.

Nevertheless, moments of brutal self-honesty was the main reason I was able to keep moving forward, albeit often at a snail's pace.

Admitting to myself that I had weak thoughts and a weak mind was tough to accept but it was also liberating.

By admitting this to myself I was starting to create a firm foundation for my life. The alternative would have been to build my life on top of a web of lies that would eventually crumble given enough time.

There are many times in my life where I feel completely and utterly lost and the only thing that has ever helped me to come unstuck is to be brutally honest with myself about where I am at.

I'm not saying this is easy, it is really hard to take an honest look at yourself, especially when there are so many distractions. But are those distractions adding to your life or are they absorbing way too much of your precious time and energy?

Look for the Real Root Cause

By taking an honest look at myself I was able to see that I was afraid to speak my mind, I was afraid of other people's judgement, and I was too easily distracted by things outside my control. Things didn't change overnight but at least I was done pretending that these were not the real issues I was dealing with.

Since I had now seen for myself that it was the opinions of other people that bothered me the most, I had a direction to move in to change things.

I identified that I felt at my most powerless to other people when I went into reaction mode so this was where I started when it came to habit formation on a mental level

How I Build Habits

Over the years, the best way I have learned to create habits is to build them slowly on top of each other over time one by one.

I used to approach habits with rigid thinking but life felt more like a chore this way.

Nowadays I like to approach habits with an experimentation mindset and a Goldilocks approach of finding just the right habit that helps improve both the quality of my life and my results.

As I look back on my journey so far there were only a few cornerstone habits that helped me to change my life for the better:

- The habit of shifting my reactions to responses.

- The habit of physical exercise at least 3 times a week.

- The habit of drinking water daily.

- The habit of reading.

- The habit of applying what I learn in the real world.

Chapter 10

Breaking the Reactive Cycle

"Be the change you want to see in the world." -
Mahatma Gandhi

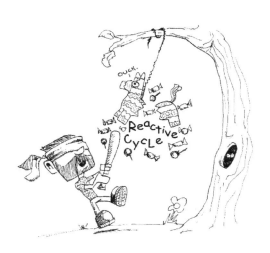

The Buck Stops Here

Anyone who has ever tried to follow a diet or tried to do more of the things that will make your life better will know how difficult it is to even get started.

While operating on a surface level thinking that your problem is solely to do with your weight or your job or your friend's circle is difficult, I have found it a lot harder to take ownership for all the bad decisions, indecisions and patterns that might not have even begun with me.

It's quite a debilitating feature of human nature that taking credit for the good comes naturally to you while taking credit for the bad is something that you won't automatically want to do. Yet, taking credit for the bad in your life is where real transformation and change come from.

If you want to start changing your life for the better today you need to take ownership for how you are right now and forget about blaming anything or anyone else for your problems. Seek solutions instead of scapegoats.

Break automatic reactions to people

The reason I chose to start breaking my reactions to people was because it was simple, straightforward and I knew it would have the biggest impact on my life at that time.

If I could manage to start breaking some of my reactive patterns, I knew more things would soon start shifting in my life too.

My realization that slowing down mentally created mental space in my mind allowed me to believe that I could use this space to start breaking patterns once I set that intention.

When you react, you give up your power to the other person but when you respond you keep your power. I wanted to keep my power.

A win for me at that time was to just become more aware of how many times I drifted into reactive mode throughout the day, what was happening, what triggered it and what I could do differently next time. It wasn't to criticise or judge it, it was simply to become more aware of it.

Subtle Mind Games and Power Dynamics

With this intention, I started to see the mind games behind some of my interactions, the subtle power dynamics as well as some of the masks I was wearing and who seemed to trigger them within me.

I noticed who I wouldn't reveal my true feelings to, I noticed the character other people brought out in me and I questioned why this was. Some of the questions that really helped me were *why does their opinion of me bother me so much?* and *why does it make sense to choose to spend my time around someone I don't fundamentally like or trust?*

I asked questions like these in an introspective way, sort of like handing them over to a higher intelligence to show me the answers that I needed to see.

The simple practical steps were to catch myself reacting, say nothing and allow the conversation to flow. Then get curious about why I was tempted to react in that manner by asking introspective questions and writing out the thoughts going through my mind.

Conscious Living

With these simple and more conscious questions, I became more aware of the quality of my relationships. Up until this point, I had largely accepted the people who happened to be in my life and I did my best to get along with them.

This often led me to not being honest about what I was interested in talking about and how I wanted to be spending my time.

It led to a habit of people-pleasing in order to fit in instead of questioning whether this was the right environment for me or if I was the right fit for the people in this environment.

Notice the urge to project blame

Once I started to gain some insights into the reality of my day to day life, one option would have been to blame some of the people in my immediate environment for triggering me.

As this is such an easy option to take, I knew that this was the sign of a weak mind. My initial brutal self-honesty was beginning to serve a purpose as I had already established my clear long-term objective to strengthen my mind, not weaken it any further.

In her research around vulnerability, Brené Brown explains that blame doesn't have any adaptive qualities to it other than to help us to discharge uncomfortable energy.

As I reflect on this in my own life, I can't remember a single instance where I blamed someone for something with it having a positive effect on their behaviour. Nor do I ever remember wanting to change for someone who pointed the finger at me rightly or wrongly.

It was all ME

When I stopped looking externally and started to take a closer look at my part in every situation, I began to notice that the patterns in my life, while seemingly all very different, had one common denominator - ME.

A simple yet utterly mind-blowing realisation for me at that time. Again, it was hard for me to accept this but once I allowed the feeling of stupid to wash over me this realisation only further fueled my belief that meaningful change was possible for me.

I no longer had to wait for the environment to change because for better or for worse I was at the epicenter of every environment I found myself in.

Self-Image – Your Inner Thermostat

As I wondered how I could have overlooked this most basic of truths I began to read more about the mind and I gradually began to gain a better understanding of how my thoughts and beliefs filter how I perceive the reality I live in.

As I began to immerse myself, I realised that it wasn't that I was stupid, I was just blinded by my own perception.

In *Psycho-Cybernetics* Robert Maxwell talks about self-image and how our mind operates like a thermostat. It only allows us to see and act according to how we see ourselves.

If you believe you're not sporty then you won't do sports unless you are motivated to challenge and debunk this idea through action. If you believe other people are always to blame for your life's problems then this is what you will see while ignoring your own part in every situation.

Embrace your shyness

For years, I had the habit of thinking that being naturally shy and reserved was a bad thing and a limitation on my potential. I thought I could either stay this way and limit myself or try to be more outgoing and talkative.

This erroneous belief influenced my actions and behaviors accordingly. I would feel annoyed if someone called me shy and I would end up talking for the sake of it just to prove those people wrong. This led to a lot of overthinking and internal conflicts in my mind.

The main fear behind all this was the fear that I would let other people dominate me, tell me who I am and always be put in my place by someone else.

What I didn't know was that the fear itself was making the very thing I resisted take form in my life.

The journey I took learning to speak French allowed me to see how what I focused on in my environment was unconsciously moudling me to see myself in a certain way. It allowed me to see my more introverted side in a more positive light.

When learning French I had to make more of an effort to engage and speak with new people more consistently. As a shy and reserved type of guy I didn't think I could do this.

I took action regardless because my motivation to learn French was stronger than my limiting belief. As I took action, I gradually began to see the benefits to not speaking for the sake of it.

In languages, if you listen more than you speak you get in more practice time than someone overly self-conscious about wanting to speak perfectly and procrastinating more often than not instead.

As I met more different types of people I began to notice that I naturally talked more when I met someone with shared interests and values or someone who I just happened to find very interesting.

I didn't have to force myself to become an extrovert. Instead, I could embrace the positive aspects to being naturally more introverted and with that, I could find my flow through life better and the people I naturally gravitated towards.

Consciously optimise your life

The key then is to optimise your life and become more conscious of situations and places where you simply survive and the situations and places where you begin to actually thrive.

Now that I was aware of this, I started to take some mental notes of the places and situations where I felt out of place and I started to gradually do less of that.

These places included being found inside a nightclub until the early hours of the morning as well as hanging out in a large group of people who didn't share similar interests to me.

In contrast to this, the situations and places where I felt most at home were hanging out in coffee shops, writing, speaking with new and interesting people, reading books, yoga, meditation and creating new projects.

The simple decision to align myself with where I naturally feel at home afforded me the opportunity to start doing all the things I enjoy doing today including my podcast and writing this book.

Idle Gossip

"Great minds discuss ideas; average minds discuss events; small minds discuss people."

- Eleanor Roosevelt

The first time I read the above quote from Eleanor Roosevelt it stopped me in my tracks. The distinction seemed so simple and yet so obvious. It opened up a door in my mind to believe that anyone could choose to become great.

My initial reaction to the thought that bubbled up inside my mind that idle gossip was a habit was skepticism. At the time I was looking for 'unconventional' ways to free up some of my time, so I could do more of the things I wanted to do.

I always assumed gossip was an inescapable part of life so I was curious to find out what results acting on the theory that idle gossip is a choice would bring.

It was very hard at first to break the habit and I frequently failed and would find myself beating myself up about it. Nevertheless, I didn't quit and I focused on the times I was able to disengage from the conversation or change topic altogether.

Again, my intention was as simple as either noticing the impulse to gossip and instead say nothing and change the topic of conversation or simply to hear the other person out.

Needless drama or some of your time back?

As the months and years went by, I found that the less I gossiped the more time I had to talk about ideas, experiment and create.

Just like in Eleanor's quote I began to see that once you start shifting your focus from talking about other people and from talking about events there is nothing much else to focus on other than talking about ideas and creating things in the world.

I also began to realise how bad a listener I was and how often I was just waiting for my turn to speak or add to the story.

As I began to gossip less, I generally felt better about myself, cared less about what other people thought of me and I experienced a huge decrease in the paranoia and drama in my life.

With this change, I noticed the compulsive liars and drama lovers gradually fade away from my life.

CHAPTER 11

A BOOK A DAY

"It is not the strongest of the species that survives, nor the most intelligent that survives. It is the one that is most adaptable to change."

- Charles Darwin

The Reading Habit

As I sat watching Tai's Tedx Talk - *Why I Read A Book a Day and Why You Should Too,* it suddenly dawned on me that reading was a habit.

What created this new connection in my brain was the analogy Tai gave as he invited the audience to come to his house this weekend to pick the brains of some of the great minds both past and present. These great minds included Mother Theresa, Mahatma Gandhi, and Bill Gates. I had never thought about books in this way before.

At the time I was on the lookout for a mentor, anyone who could fill my head with knowledge and help me find the right path. While I was on the lookout for someone a few steps ahead of me I had completely overlooked the fact that books could bridge the gap right now. Books have the added benefit that they force the writer to really reflect on and think about the key lessons they learned in their life that transformed them from ordinary to great.

I started to read Gandhi with the intention of discovering insights into self-mastery and books from entrepreneurs such as Elon Musk and Steve Jobs to gain some insights into how successful businesses are created in the real world.

Mental Models

The concept of reading a book a day was completely foreign to me at this point. It took me back to the trouble I had assimilating the concept of speaking a foreign language from day 1 when I first discovered language hacking.

The problem came from the fact that I was trying to use my existing mental model of looking at the world to make sense of a completely new concept. A concept that represented a paradigm shift in my thinking when it came to reading books.

When Tai says he reads a book a day he isn't saying he reads it cover to cover. He has his own method that works for him which involves skimming through the summary and chapters of the book and picking out a few chapters to read.

He sees himself as a gold miner mining for golden nuggets. His belief is that most books really only contain one or two golden nuggets.

The idea of reading a book like this at first felt odd to me. I wasn't taught to think about books in this way at school so it felt really uncomfortable to entertain a new way of thinking about books.

When was the last time you heard a teacher ask a student to skim a textbook, pick out the most important things from it and test it in their life? Chances are never but these are the type of skills we need to develop for the real world as adults.

Associate discomfort with growth

We are no longer children or teenagers stuck inside an outdated and often times redundant system. We can choose to let our minds wander and break out of this fixed way of thinking about learning whenever we make that decision.

It isn't always easy but learning to associate discomfort with growth has helped me to persist and break through many of my self-imposed mental limitations.

When you really stop and think about it, how much of the information in those academic textbooks did you retain after school was done testing you on it?

I have learned the hard way that without a conscious application of knowledge the knowledge remains pretty meaningless.

The key to understanding anything

At first, I wondered how someone could actually make sense of what the book was really about if they were reading it this quickly.

As I developed the habit of reading, I came to realize that this method makes sense, at least for nonfiction books.

After reading well over a hundred books across multiple different disciplines over a 3 year period I have come to see recurring patterns, peppered with some new insights here and there.

Patterns such as active learning being a core component of how we naturally learn as human beings. Tai Lopez (marketing), Benny Lewis (foreign languages) and Jon Sonmez (computer programming) all mention this as one of their cornerstone philosophies that have helped them to get ahead in an ever-changing world.

Taking the gold miner approach to reading books allows you to apply and test things in the real world at an accelerated rate as you choose to only pay attention to what is most relevant to you at each step in the process.

This is when the true latent power of knowledge is unlocked like an oyster just waiting for you to open it and find the pearl.

Real World Understanding = Knowledge + Application

So that's where I began. I started with the book titles you can find available in the books section on Tai Lopez's website.

These books span many different topics including history, philosophy, psychology, and business. If you want some answers to your life this is the place I would recommend you to start.

Biographies

I eventually started to read biographies and autobiographies. These books helped me to gain insights into the general journey that successful people go on and the patterns and principles that these stories are built around.

I learned how the media bias will make you overlook and ignore the years of hard work and sacrifice that goes into the 'overnight success'.

I began to see people such as Elon Musk and Steve Jobs as fallible human beings just like you and I, with real emotions and motivations that were often born out of pain.

It humanized these people in a way that simply observing them on a tv screen or in a magazine can't quite manage to do. These books gave me access to some of the inner thoughts and dialogues that shaped their lives.

Some of these thoughts aren't sensational enough to see the light of day in mainstream media but profound enough to transform your life if you let them. It also helped me to gain some insights into the immense human potential locked up inside all of us.

CHAPTER 12

REWIRE YOUR BRAIN

"Life isn't about finding yourself. Life is about creating yourself." - George Bernard Shaw

The 67 Steps

When I first stumbled upon Tai Lopez, I must admit that I was a little skeptical and dubious, probably because of his infamous Lamborghini video. I think up until that point, I never purchased anything where there was a substantial amount of people saying it was a scam.

Purchasing his 67 steps program and ignoring the naysayers helped to reinforce the invaluable lesson to trust my own intuition and remain open to learning my own lessons.

The aim of the course is to help you rewire your brain to create positive and lasting change in your life by downloading ideas from the great minds both past and present.

The number of days for the program comes from research done by Phillipa Lally, of the University College of London, in a study published by the European Journal of Social Psychology, which found that it takes on average 66 days to form a new habit. Tai threw in 1 day for good measure.

The course consisted of one video per day. This was the next habit I began to incorporate into my life. I learned so much from this course about human psychology, success and evolutionary theory. The biggest lesson I took away from this course was from Charles Darwin where I learned that no matter the species adaptability in life is the most important thing.

Cognitive Biases

I first became aware of the cognitive biases from the 67 Steps. Great investors such as Warren Buffet, Charlie Munger and Ray Dalio all talk about ways to minimize the effects of their own brain's cognitive biases.

Becoming aware of the cognitive biases was another thing that greatly enhanced the quality of my life.

This awareness helped to shed more light on the fact that my brain has a distorted perception of reality when left unchecked. It's my job to minimise these biases, so I can make better life choices.

The authority misinfluence tendency helped to explain my natural tendency to follow instruction just because it comes from someone in a position of 'authority'. The social proof tendency helped to explain why my automatic tendency is to think and act the same as the people around me even if it doesn't feel right to me. The inconsistency avoidance tendency helped to explain my aversion to change.

For a list and description of the 25 most common cognitive biases check out *The Psychology of Human Misjudgment.*

CHAPTER 13

I WILL BE HAPPY WHEN...

"We spend money we do not have, on things we do not need, to impress people who don't care." - Will Smith

Bullshit Stories

As long as you're believing some form of bullshit story, you will remain stuck. Between 2014 and 2016, I decided to put in the work to get smarter in an effort to free myself from the bullshit stories controlling my life at both a conscious and an unconscious level.

I was tired of taking opinions at face value simply because I didn't have the language and understanding to outright reject them from entering my mind.

Opinions such as 'nobody loves their job' and 'everybody hates Mondays' and fixed realities such as the economy determines your lot in life. I was sick and tired of hearing these whiny repetitive and never-ending narratives play out inside my mind.

Internalizing such a fixed view of the world proved to be extremely toxic to me. What was worse was that I knew I was living with limitations other people had created.

For too long I had left my mind wide open to internalizing other people's beliefs, opinions and limitations. It was time to really start changing this.

Let's Talk about Ideas

Towards the end of 2015, I noticed that I was starting to engage in more conversations centered around ideas and in turn attracting more people into my life who were forward-thinking and looking at possibilities instead of lack and limitation. This was a small but very encouraging sign for me.

When my focus was on lack and limitation, I had the habit of comparing myself to others, do what everyone else was doing just to fit in, overly fear being judged and pay way too much attention to the news and other things that were outside my control. It was a massive win to start shifting away from and having less of these experiences in my life.

Nevertheless, I noticed that my day to day feelings about myself remained largely unaltered. This wasn't the first time I became aware of this disconnect. I first became aware of this on my journey to becoming a polyglot.

Prior to this, I had assumed that if I could speak multiple languages, I would have much more self-confidence and generally feel better about myself. That was the logic coming from my head on an intellectual level but once I achieved my goal my feelings about myself didn't shift at all.

Infinite Loops

When nothing shifted on an emotional level, I noticed that my unconscious tendency was to set an even bigger goal and live out the exact same pattern all over again. I began to refer to this as the 'I will be happy when...' loop.

It isn't hard to see this pattern play out in the education system where the implied message in people's actions and behaviours go along the lines of 'I will be happy when I pass my exams... graduate... get a job'.

Very rarely do you see actions and behaviours that reveal a student content with where they are right now and with a genuine excitement to learn more.

The Whack-a-Mole Illusion

From taking a step back and observing how we tend to approach the traditional milestones in our lives like graduation, our first job, our first promotion, the expectation almost feels like each milestone will remove a weight off our mind and will somehow make us feel happy.

The truth of the matter for me was that once one milestone was reached it wasn't long before I had my eyes firmly set on the next one. The goalposts kept shifting but my expectation that the milestone would bring me some sort of long-term relief or a deeper sense of contentment took a lot longer to shift.

It was almost like I was living my life playing an endless game of whack-a-mole. I had never really taken the time to question this assumption, largely because I didn't even know it was playing out in my life, at the time it just looked like life to me.

CHAPTER 14

A NEUTRAL WORLD

"Everything we hear is an opinion, not a fact. Everything we see is a perspective, not the truth." - Marcus Aurelius

Breaking the Pattern

Once I was aware of this 'I will be happy when...' loop, I knew I no longer wanted it to continue to control my life.

I wouldn't have been able to tell you at that time what exactly needed to change, I just knew something didn't feel right. There was a disconnect between how I was living and how I wanted to live.

I knew that I wanted to spend more of my time creating things for the sheer joy and challenge of it, I wanted to have a sense of meaning, purpose, and direction in my life and I wanted to be surrounded by genuine and relentlessly optimistic people.

With the exception of writing, I wasn't taking a whole lot of action, largely because of my fears. I felt like an imposter when it came to trying something new and I hated the idea of really putting myself out there and giving an honest attempt only to fail and embarrass myself in the process.

Focus on the Process

At this time, I was almost purely outcome-focused. I didn't see the value of focusing on the process and setting process-based goals. This magnified the idea of public failure being one of the worst things imaginable to me and reinforced the 'I will be happy when...' loop.

With a focus on the process and on personal growth, I was starting to see that win or lose is a perspective.

When you stop seeking external validation for everything that you do you begin to see that life has been handing you win or grow scenarios. With this shift in mindset, I was beginning to break the 'I will be happy when...' loop.

I still had a lot to learn about the patterns playing out in my life on an emotional level. So, faced with an unknown unknown I decided that I needed to drastically change my approach.

I knew that I was at one of those junctures and what got me here wouldn't necessarily get me to the next level. So, I began to do something I hadn't done before. I began to read up on the more abstract fields like quantum physics and stoic philosophy.

Stoic Philosophy

I had previously read books on psychology and philosophy which gradually led me to stoicism. The biggest takeaway I took from stoicism is that the world is neutral but for the meaning that I give it.

This was a fundamentally different thought to what I was used to entertaining. If you are living in the Western world and take a look at the world around you today it's easy to see that most people don't tend to look at the world in this way.

It wasn't much of a stretch for me to see that I was trained to look at the world in the way that most people traditionally tend to look at it today.

Most people seem to attach a very specific and concrete meaning to an event and tend to underplay or outright dismiss their own perception of the event.

Reading about the anomalies that frequently emerge from eye witness testimonies would suggest that our perception has a huge influence on what we see.

My automatic impulse is to overlook the role my perception plays. Initially, it felt counterintuitive to consider that the meaning might be coming from me rather than the event itself.

However, my experience with psychosis taught me that I don't live in an entirely objective world. This experience allowed me to entertain and begin to internalize the ideas contained within stoicism.

After all one of the people who lived by a stoic philosophy was Marcus Aurelius, a Roman Emperor and General, if he could see the neutrality in the world around him in the day to day circumstances he was faced with then I could at least open my mind to it.

CHAPTER 15

ONLINE LEARNING

"You never change things by fighting against the existing reality. To change something, build a new model that makes the old model obsolete." - Buckminster Fuller

Opening My Eyes to Social Media

Living with psychosis and having access to social media was a complete and utter nightmare. As I sat scrolling through past conversations, I was beginning to see different meanings and perspectives emerge everywhere.

Where once I would look at a message from one innocent point of view, my brain was now beginning to distort my perception and look for bad intentions in the messages I had received over the years from different people.

I was beginning to see frenemies for the first time and I was beginning to see that maybe the things I had fobbed off as someone 'messing' were actually them saying what they really thought.

Switching my Social Media Brain Off and On

After a rollercoaster ride of confusion, I took a break from social media believing it to be the source of my problems.

A few months later I came back to social media. As I did, I began to realise that social media wasn't the issue. The issue was human dysfunction. As I was beginning to come to terms with my own dysfunction, I started to look for the possibilities that social media offers instead of the problems.

I shifted from passively using social media to more consciously creating on it instead. The name for my podcast 'The Happy Mindset' comes from a Facebook page and the simple desire to share the things I was learning that were having a positive impact on my life.

My hypothesis was that Facebook is a neutral tool, you can either use it to engage with and fuel negativity or you can use it to share and spread realness and positivity.

The Technological Revolution

In my formative years, I didn't have access to the world wide web as it exists today. I was in primary school when I remember seeing my first computer. I didn't find it all that interesting, just a bunch of Word documents and a teacher who helped us to do some basic searches.

All throughout my formal education, right up until I graduated university, I didn't see computers in the same way I see them now. It didn't really occur to me that you could use these machines to self-educate and transform your life.

I saw them purely as a way to either do research for an assignment or as a way to procrastinate and kill some time. Granted technology looked a lot different back then, so it was much easier to overlook the immense possibility at my fingertips.

But technology has changed the game forever. You no longer need to live in ignorance or based on someone else's belief system. You can exercise your power of choice whenever you want.

If you aren't satisfied with the status quo in your current environment then you can use the internet as a superhighway to connect you with new people, ideas and beliefs. Ideas and beliefs that have the power to help you understand yourself better and to tap into more of your true potential.

I believe that if you have a strong enough why then you will always find a way to make your visions and dreams become a reality but without the internet, I know my journey would have been a lot longer and a lot more tedious.

Mind Valley

So, the next major step in my self-directed education was the inclusion of online courses. Mind Valley was the first platform I signed up to that was a little bit different from what I was used to.

Prior to taking courses at Mind Valley, I had been using platforms like Udemy, Udacity, Khan Academy and Lynda. The founder of Mind Valley is Vishen Lakhiani. I liked Vishen's story and it felt like he had a sense of purpose and direction in his life, that was exactly what I was looking for.

A Pinch is Helpful but not the whole Jar

As I was taking these steps my biggest obstacle came in the form of my own cynicism. I think a pinch of cynicism is healthy and can help to keep you firmly grounded in reality. However, somewhere along the line I had picked up a large jar of cynicism and carried it around like a dead weight around my neck.

My cynicism about the world around me largely came from my belief that if something looks too good to be true then it is. With this belief, I either overlooked anything that looked too positive or I took a close enough look until I found something I didn't like, so I could reaffirm my self-limiting belief.

Looking at life through this lens was easy. It meant I would never be disappointed because I never had to open my mind to entertaining something new. In my eyes, I never looked foolish because I would never attempt something I wasn't sure I would succeed at.

The Illusion of Certainty

However, the flipside of buying into the illusion of certainty was that I became more fearful about the world around me. I was less spontaneous, more predictable and generally had less experiences and frames of reference to draw upon to deepen my understanding of the world and the people around me.

Thankfully I didn't wait until I was cured of my cynicism to go ahead and open my mind to studying at Mind Valley. I chose to take action despite feeling uncomfortable and uncertain about what was in store for me.

Disillusionment & Brules

Vishen took his first steps on his journey to creating Mind Valley when he found himself feeling miserable after he landed his first software engineering job at Microsoft. I could immediately relate to his sense of disillusionment between what the world tells us will make us happy and what actually makes us happy.

His book *The Code of the Extraordinary Mind* allowed me to gain some further insights into how Vishen perceived the world. I really resonated with his word 'Brule' which was a term he coined to describe a bullshit rule.

He used this word to shine a light on some of the ludicrous beliefs that we take on from our early childhood, our culture and the people around us without ever really taking the time to challenge these beliefs as we mature and develop as adults.

Learning can Actually Improve Your Life

The courses at Mind Valley helped to open my mind to tantra, the power of the human mind and diet. I never would have expected that I would come to learn about tantra.

During this time, I was beginning to acquire a better understanding of why immersing yourself in a wide variety of diverse fields can prove to be invaluable because it teaches you the art of learning and how to look for patterns. For more on this way of thinking about learning check out *The First 20 Hours by Josh Kaufman.*

During this time, I started to realise that you can learn for pleasure. I also had a greater appreciation for the vast amount of things I could learn about.

Up until my early 20's I associated the word learning with dry textbooks, passing exams and an obligation. In my 20's my understanding of learning changed to being an opportunity and included learning about myself and the universe.

Transition from Online to Real World

I spent a couple of months engaging in the courses at Mind Valley in my spare time but eventually, there came a point where I wanted to transition from online education to real-world education. It was around this time that I first became aware of Multi-Level Marketing (MLM's).

My interactions with my first MLM was another new, uncomfortable but very interesting experience for me. Personal development was a large component to what they were doing and it was of a high energy Tony Robbins variety of personal development where I really felt like a fish out of water.

The MLM was created around a core passion of mine - travel. Although I didn't travel much in my 20's, because I spent almost all of my savings on my self-education, I love getting an opportunity to travel and meet new people. This combined with the prospect of creating a side income was enough for me to give it a chance. After a few months of dipping my toe in the water, I realised it didn't fully align with what I wanted to do and the impact I wanted to have in the world.

OK – I'm willing to Put Myself Out There

My key takeaway from this experience was that I was willing to take the necessary steps to really move outside my comfort zone but it had to be something I fully believed in and it had to come from within me. This became my non-negotiable for moving forward.

When I made the decision to quit the MLM it wasn't long before I came across a Meetup in Dublin that mentioned Bob Proctor. I had stumbled across Mind Valley from listening to some of Bob Proctor's videos and I had kind of forgotten about Bob in the process.

Chapter 16

Moving Outside My Comfort Zone

"The illiterate of the 21st century are not those who cannot read or write but those who cannot learn, unlearn and relearn." -Alvin Toffler

Self-Help and Personal Development

Whenever I thought of the words personal development or self-help, I felt uncomfortable. I was drawn to this field but I knew nothing about it.

I didn't have close friends who talked about personal development. I had this fear that this world might consume me if I wasn't careful enough. That I might somehow lose myself and become someone I'm not. I dreaded the thought of friends and family referring to me as the guy living in cloud cuckoo land with his head in the clouds.

Despite the numerous mental and emotional blocks, I had around the words personal development and self-help, I found myself listening to people who were in this space.

I started listening to people like Bob Proctor, Eric Thomas, Les Brown, Lewis Howes, Marie Forleo, Jay Shetty, Jim Rohn, and other motivational and insightful people. I wanted to listen to people who thought in terms of possibility rather than lack and limitation. I wanted this type of mindset to start rubbing off on me.

Take something from everyone

At this time, I was also learning to take something from everyone, an idea I internalized from the 67 Steps Program. Up until taking the

67 Steps, I held a very rigid way of looking at the world.

Without knowing it I believed that someone was either good or bad but that they couldn't be both. I also found it difficult to really learn from someone who didn't meet my standards of the 'perfect' person.

"Either you are a Victim in life - a sucker or a loser who's always being taken advantage of and can't hold their own - or you're a VIKING - someone who sees the threat of being victimized as a constant, so you stay in control, you dominate, you exert your power over other things, and you never show vulnerability."
-Brene Brown

From reading Brené Brown's work, I realized that the mental model I was largely perceiving the world through was very much dominated by the lens of victim or viking.

This wasn't hard to understand, I largely lived unconscious to how my environment was moulding me.

Living unaware to the effect mass media was having on me left my mind wide open to perceive the world as a very negative and hostile place to live in. The implied messages of good people versus bad people, the need to remain afraid to remain safe, these are just some of the implicit messages that I left my mind open to receiving and my body to internalising on a daily basis.

From Fear to Curiosity

Taking the 67 Steps Program was when I made a conscious decision to become curious about the world around me. I was no longer willing to accept things to be newsworthy or relevant simply because they appeared on a television screen or in the paper.

I decided to live more consciously and immerse myself in resources that could empower me instead of trap me. These resources included books, courses, and videos which I consumed in vast quantities in an effort to feed and nourish both my mind and my soul.

There is a well-known saying in the computer programming world 'garbage in, garbage out'. I took this to heart and I decided that my mind would no longer be left wide open to accepting unnecessary negativity bordering on complete and utter nonsense.

My personal development mistranslation

Attending webinars and online events were among the first steps on my path to entering into the personal development world. The transition to real-world events brought up a new set of uncomfortable emotions which washed over me like a tsunami of uncomfortable questions.

What if someone sees me here? and *who are these people anyway?* These were just some of the types of questions swirling through my mind as I sat uncomfortably at these events among a bunch of people I didn't know from Adam five minutes earlier.

To add fuel to the fire I judged myself for entertaining these thoughts. I naively believed that aiming to think positive all the time was what personal development was all about.

I would later realise that this misperception was the main source of my uncomfortable feelings with the words personal development. I felt like the ultimate imposter as I sat there thinking to myself if only they knew the types of thoughts whirling through my head then they wouldn't want me here.

Order out of Chaos

Despite all this internal confusion I managed to go to a few meetups and with each event, I got more comfortable with feeling like an idiot and a fish out of water.

Instead of always looking for the path of least resistance I was taking another step towards training my mind to start taking the path of most resistance.

The information I was being exposed to was helping me to gradually understand my emotions, my thoughts and my mind at a deeper level.

I was learning that any problem I was experiencing in my life always began with me. This allowed me to take increased ownership for my life instead of believing I was a victim to circumstance.

Before attending these events and immersing myself in this world I had believed that it was other people's opinions of personal development that was the reason I felt uncomfortable about it.

It was only through consistently showing up to these events, taking courses and reading books that I began to realise that the discomfort came from my own belief system. My beliefs were the only thing that was gradually changing and this shift is what was transmuting chaos into order in my mind.

As I began to understand the very things that had me sitting there in fear, anxiety and overwhelm the uncomfortable emotions became less and less of an issue. I began to see for perhaps the first time that I wasn't the only one completely lost and I wasn't the only one lacking in understanding.

Lessons from Bob

*"We think in secret, and it comes to pass,
environment is but our looking glass'"*

- James Allen

Bob Proctor speaks a lot about the Laws of the Universe and the mind. One of the major insights I got from his work was that you don't get rid of the cold by fighting it, instead, you light a fire and focus on the heat which will eliminate the cold.

This reinforced my theory that where you focus your attention is everything, instead of fighting what you don't want, focus on what you do want.

Two other key takeaways I took from my time studying his material were that the subconscious mind thinks in pictures and if I want to be free I have got to be me.

Invest in Yourself

In 2016, after attending a number of different meetups and workshops I decided it was time to commit to up leveling my life, achieve new results and perceive the world differently.

Warren Buffet, one of the richest men in the world is often quoted as saying - *'the most important investment you can make is in yourself'* and this is what I chose to do.

I took Bob's Thinking Into Results program. At the time this was a huge investment for me and I wasn't entirely sure what I was looking to get from this program but I knew I wanted some sort of change.

The idea of taking this program made me feel uncomfortable which was a sure sign of major resistance. This was the biggest financial investment I had made in myself and it really pushed and stretched me outside my comfort zone.

Through this program, I began to see the value of challenging and shifting my limiting beliefs through taking action. I began to understand the immense power and simplicity of the mind.

I began to see the excuses my brain was making up on the spot to stop me from moving forward. There were exercises on focus and visualization along with different affirmations. This program helped me to take increased personal ownership for my life and it helped to simplify my life.

Still Something Missing..

At this time, I was still living with the mindset of looking for the 'correct answer', that one size fits all and an understanding of what actually works and what doesn't.

I didn't know I was living with this mindset then and it would take another few years before I would see I was living with it but I am so glad to be more conscious of it now.

Unconsciously living with this mindset alone was enough to keep me stuck in seeking mode and unnecessary mental suffering.

While I was gaining a deeper understanding of the power of the mind, action, and habit I was beginning to sense that something was missing for me on a personal level.

It still felt like my self-worth was dependent on achieving these big results I was setting for myself. This didn't entirely sit well with me.

Don't get me wrong I want to achieve bigger and better results, but I don't want the results to come with a lack of perspective on the bigger picture or a feeling of misalignment.

My mental health had suffered once before so this time I wanted to engage in a more holistic approach even if it meant that I would have to take a more long-term approach to finding real success and happiness.

CHAPTER 17

CHALLENGE YOUR LIMITING BELIEFS

"How can you achieve your 10-year plan in the next 6 months?" - Peter Thiel

Assumptions & Limiting Beliefs

I didn't know what limiting beliefs were until I challenged myself to learn Spanish and Italian in 6 months in 2010. The idea of learning two languages this quickly meant that I had to fundamentally rethink everything I thought I knew about language learning.

By forcing myself to think differently I discovered word usage frequency, I questioned the traditional cycle of studying 'beginner', 'intermediate' and 'advanced' materials and I came across new concepts such as speaking from Day 1.

Once I got to conversational fluency in both languages within 3 months, I started to realise that the only thing preventing me from doing this earlier were my own self-imposed limitations.

The material existed on the internet long before I became aware of it and it wasn't that I had somehow managed to get 10x smarter in the space of 3 months.

Transferable Skills

Coding initially caught my attention because of two self-limiting beliefs. In 2014 I met William who at the time was self-learning to code.

Two things immediately struck me about this. I had always assumed you couldn't just teach yourself to code by following online tutorials and building projects and expect to get a real job out of this. The education system had conditioned me to buy into the idea that a computer science degree was the most basic requirement necessary.

The second reason was that he said 'you don't need to be a math genius...'. At the time I believed that coding was purely mathematical and science-based and had nothing at all to do with linguistics.

Break out of your conditioned worldview

Again, the answer was staring me right in the face 'computer programming language' but when you're conditioned to look at the world in a certain way you tend to miss the blatantly obvious.

These two assumptions combined with my experience self-learning Spanish and Italian meant that I shifted my focus from learning human languages to computer languages.

Landing a job fixing computers and going from the least likely to fix a computer in my family to the go-to guy again showed to me the power of self-belief.

While writing this book I finally transitioned into a software developer role which allowed me to enter into yet another world beyond my mental barriers.

Up until the point that I got curious about computer programming and building websites,

I had always associated these things with highly intelligent geeks lacking in social skills.

Rethinking how I perceived foreign languages and computer programming led me to wondering what other limiting assumptions I was making about myself and the world around me.

Soft Skills

The first book that opened my mind to the world of soft skills was *The Charisma Myth* by Olivia Fox Cabane. To be honest, I hadn't put a lot of thought into how personality traits develop. At the time I wasn't even aware that soft skills were really a thing you could work on.

I wasn't taught about the distinction between hard skills and soft skills at school. I had always assumed that people had fixed personalities.

I hadn't put a lot of thought into how these personalities developed in the first place. I assumed that things like charisma, being likable and being outgoing were all-natural innate qualities that you either did or didn't possess.

As I became more aware of the importance of soft skills, I began to see it mentioned more often. I noticed that it was talked about in the computer programming world as the key difference between a successful freelancer and an unsuccessful one. Sure, you needed good technical skills but without soft skills, you were at sea without a paddle.

I saw developing soft skills as not only a matter of gathering new information and practicing new techniques, I also sensed that a large part of developing soft skills came from breaking free of self-limiting beliefs.

Who am I really?

In hindsight whenever I have made a significant shift in my life my belief system has also shifted. It isn't just a matter of gathering all the 'correct' information, if that were the case the most successful and fulfilled people would be those who know the most.

In reality, the people who know a lot intellectually or think they know a lot are quite often tortured souls.

My beliefs about who I was and what I was and wasn't capable of doing needed to be fundamentally altered. As I started to look in this direction, I started to pay more attention to my relationship with my thoughts.

Chapter 18

Be Here Now

"I have realised that the past and the future are real illusions, that they exist in the present, which is what there is and all there is."

- *Alan Watts*

Meditation

I used meditation as a way to delve deeper into my mind and discover my relationship with my thoughts.

Before I began the meditation habit in 2016 I had very little distance from my thoughts. With this lack of distance and perspective meditation felt really uncomfortable.

If you look at meditation objectively how hard can it be? It's basically a human being sitting in silence. A human being just being.

The only thing that could possibly make it difficult would be the types of thoughts bubbling up from within.

Weeding out my misperceptions

I used to completely overlook meditation. I thought it was reserved for biblical and enlightened people. Growing up Jesus was the only person I had heard of who actively meditated. I didn't want people to think I had a Messiah complex by saying that I now meditated too.

All of these were misperceptions and tricks of my own mind. For one, I discovered that I didn't have to tell anyone I meditated or turn it into some sort of weird competition. I wasn't doing it to enhance my sense of self, I was doing it for my own peace of mind.

Coming from this intention, what meditation turned out to be for me was an opportunity to sit with my thoughts. By sitting with them I was able to shine a light on some of the madness going through my mind on a daily basis.

I started to see that that madness wasn't me. I had always assumed it was up until I discovered meditation. The act of meditation also gave me access to a better sense of what the flow state feels like in my day to day life.

I started to gain some distance and perspective from some of my most limiting and self-conscious thoughts. This distance and perspective allow me to take a step back quicker when I am living with a revved-up mind in my day to day.

I started by using guided meditations on the Head Space app for 10 minutes a day. The act of meditating was an unknown for me but I knew that consistency and a focus on the process would help me to persevere.

Uncomfortable Questions

In the first few weeks thoughts that emerged for me included *who do you think you are meditating?* and *what would <insert person's name> think of you if they saw you?*

These were very uncomfortable thoughts to sit with. In my day to day life, these were the types of thoughts and emotions I was unconsciously trying to avoid by not trying new things or by being the real me.

It took a good few weeks for me to begin to realise that some of these thoughts were coming from my own mind and not from the people I was imagining judging me in those moments.

Fool Me Twice, Shame on Me

This is how powerful the mind is and how easily it can fool you. I was sitting in my bedroom by myself for 10 minutes a day and in those moments when those feelings and thoughts emerged my initial reaction was to run for the hills.

It was strange for me to start seeing that what I was really afraid of all this time were some of my own unrecognised thoughts.

Thoughts are slippery, and the mind can be incredibly deceptive but by taking it step by step one day at a time I have been able to gradually break free of my most limiting and debilitating thoughts.

Looking back over my 20's my biggest strength has been my relentless persistence, even if something doesn't look like it's working if it still feels aligned to me, I don't give up on it.

Even if I am moving at a snail's pace I have realised that moving your life in the right direction is more than half the battle.

Meditate to take your Power back

The biggest benefit meditation brought to my life was that it was another medium that helped me take more of my power and life energy back.

Prior to meditating a large portion of my energy was still fixated on circumstances, people and situations that were entirely outside of my control.

With meditation, I made the decision to intentionally block out the outside world. When you do this there is nobody else to take ownership for your thoughts and emotions but yourself.

Initially, that's a scary realisation but it's also the realisation that will slowly take the negative charge out of your most limiting thoughts and emotions and start moving you on your own unique path.

The next time you find yourself procrastinating about doing the inner work you know will improve your life, ask yourself if it's simply a fear of facing yourself? Then do the work anyway.

CHAPTER 19

THE SPACE

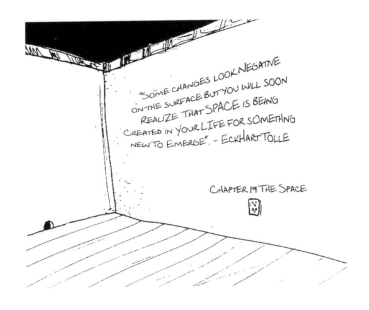

"SOME CHANGES LOOK NEGATIVE ON THE SURFACE BUT YOU WILL SOON REALIZE THAT SPACE IS BEING CREATED IN YOUR LIFE FOR SOMETHING NEW TO EMERGE". – ECKHART TOLLE

CHAPTER 19 THE SPACE

The Shift from Positive Thinking

As I browsed through the books on the bookshelf in a Cardiff airport newsagents, I had the sudden impulse to purchase a random book. It's not the first time this has happened, I am a sucker for synchronicities.

I think that synchronicities and things that seem to happen as if by chance make life a much more colourful, interesting and exciting place.

After reading the cover of a handful of books, a purple one suddenly caught my attention. The title simply read - *Results* by Jamie Smart.

I was coming back from my friend Dan's birthday weekend in Swansea and the question that was on my mind was *what am I fundamentally overlooking when it comes to understanding how my mind works?*

At the time I was gravitating towards positive thinking. I thought that it was my own bullshit stories that made me feel uneasy about positive thinking. My perception of positive thinking at this time was that it was about always focusing on the positives and blocking out the negatives.

To an extent, a focus on positive thinking worked for me. The flipside, however, was that I felt my mind was resisting the negatives just as much as it was trying to focus on the positives. I judged myself for having negative thoughts in my head and in doing so I was making things more difficult for myself.

I mean what is the point in striving to create a 'perfect' life if I can't accept who I am? In my understanding having negative thoughts is a part of who I am.

What matters most is not the specific thoughts in your head but how you choose to interact with them. The thoughts you choose to act on will eventually become manifest in your reality given enough time.

If you are wondering whether you are resisting negative thoughts right now then pay attention to how you are using your mind to move you forward.

When negative thoughts and stories come up for you do you tend to resist them and block them out or are you able to accept them and continue to focus your attention on taking action and finding solutions?

Do you feel like you are straining to get somewhere or do you feel grounded and centered as you move forward?

I thought all the answers would come from how I thought about myself and the world around me.

From the courses, I was taking and some of the books I was reading I was beginning to think that building a positive self-image was vital to leading a happy and successful life.

Self-image – the answer or a nicer looking prison?

I thought that a positive self-image was the difference between the people who were being their best selves and living life to the full and the people who settled for average.

But something didn't sit quite right with me at this time about positive thinking, affirmations and creating a better self-image. I felt like a fraud and like I was trying to pretend to be someone I wasn't.

I felt like it all hinged on how other people perceived me and a life dependent on other people's perceptions of me felt more like a life of imprisonment.

I thought there was something amiss about needing to create a self-image in the first place but I couldn't yet put my finger on it.

It felt like papering over the cracks to me in much the same way that I knew staying on medication would only numb the real pain of first taking an honest look at my life and what was really going on beneath the surface before I did anything else.

Tip of the Iceberg

Although my shift in thinking to looking at life through the lens of a growth mindset had dramatically improved my quality of thinking and how I felt about myself, I had the sense that this was only the tip of a much deeper iceberg.

Books like *The Power of Now* by Eckhart Tolle seemed like they were pointing to something much deeper than positive thinking. But I thought that maybe Eckhart and these new-age spiritual teachers were outliers and the rest of us 'normal' people would have to find something more real world.

I wasn't aware of it then but all the changes that had happened in my mind up until this point had all began with a space and that was what Eckhart and others were pointing to, the space beneath the words.

The Space Beneath the Words

In the Western world, our mind isn't conditioned to interpret or make sense of empty space. I had no idea that there was empty space underneath the mental chatter of my conditioned mind.

I don't think the existence of the space between my thoughts was some sort of secret the world kept from me. With the contrast between how I live now and how I used to live; I can see that my conditioned mind wouldn't have sat still long enough to become curious about the nature of the thoughts in my head.

The thoughts that I had identified with for so long that they had the power to do immense psychological damage to me.

Be Consistent – or else!

Looking back, it was like I had someone following me around with a gun to my head telling me to act in a certain way and to make sure I was consistent about it.

Part of my fixed identity was wrapped around being likable to other people and to fit in with their version of normal. This identity alone was a recipe for disaster.

All this was unconscious of course, it wasn't like I was walking around repeating mantras to myself like *I must be liked by others*. It has only been through taking a real hard and honest look at my habits, actions, and behaviours that I began to see for myself some of the questions and assumptions built in.

Just take an honest look

If you are looking for mental freedom and to break free of limiting patterns then start by taking an honest look at yourself.

I had gone through enough mental pain and suffering to do that and this is when I started interrupting my stories allowing space to emerge for new types of thoughts to break through.

When I was living fully immersed in my conditioned mind all I knew is that I would feel uncomfortable around other people if there was a lull in conversation for an extended period of time.

I didn't know it was the mental chatter inside my own head that was making me feel uncomfortable, I thought it was the situation itself.

I didn't know I could accept and ignore the mental chatter inside my mind coming from questions and statements like *why is everyone quiet?*, *this is weird*, *they think you're weird*, *say something*. There was little to no space in my mind to notice my captivity to this sheer and utter madness was optional.

I'm not saying that this option is easy. Some of these thought patterns and stories have been running inside my mind for literally decades and were completely unrecognizable to me until I saw some of them.

It all begins with a firm decision that you will start to break free and that your mental clarity and peace of mind is important to you.

The World Exists in Outer Space

Creating space in your mind is subtle and if you are anything like me you won't know entirely what you are doing or if it's really making a difference.

Take a moment and look around you and just focus on the empty space that makes up your world. Does this feel strange to you? I mean what are you even supposed to be looking at?

Credit: Gordn Johnson on Pixabay

The first time I saw the above image I only saw two faces. It took another person to tell me there was also a vase in there for me to focus on the empty space and see it for myself.

The outside world as a mirror for the inner

Mental space is just as subtle and invisible as the empty space we are surrounded by every single day. Our human mind cannot comprehend or conceptualise empty space so we take it for

140

granted or even ignore the fact that it is even there.

But what would our world look like if there weren't any empty space to connect everything together?

It would look chaotic and that is what a mind without any space looks and feels like too. When space begins to emerge then some order and even logic can emerge from what was once chaotic and overwhelming.

The Initial Point of Real Transformation

I completely overlooked the fact that gaining distance from my thoughts was where the transformation in my mind all began. It was minimal at first but the space has grown larger over time as I have gotten a better feel for what it is.

The space is what allowed me to become more aware of my self-talk, which allowed me to become more aware of my questions and assumptions which helped to shift me from a fixed mindset to a growth mindset.

The growth mindset pushed me outside my comfort zones to further allow my mind to expand. Meditation, self-reflection and becoming more conscious of the language I used further allowed me to create more space between myself and my thoughts.

Subtractive Psychology

This has only started to make more sense to me in retrospect. In November 2016 *Results* was about to open my mind to a better understanding of the space that helped me to break free from my chaotic thinking.

I was about 2 years into my reading habit by the time I picked up *Results*. As I was reading this book, I began to realise that there was something different about it.

Up until this book I had approached psychology and personal development with the same mindset I had for learning technical skills. My approach was additive, I was always looking for more information or the latest tool or technique.

This approach was beginning to grate on me as it was beginning to feel never-ending and overwhelming. This book however seemed to be spelling out a fundamentally different approach to psychology - a subtractive model instead of an additive one.

Connection to Source

What I gathered from this book was that the key to connecting with my well-being came from reconnecting with who I am underneath all the thinking.

Instead of adding positive affirmations or needing to change my state of mind in other artificial ways this book allowed me to begin making the shift towards noticing the space behind my very thoughts and words.

Don't ask me how but this book had somehow finally helped to open up my mind just enough to get a glimpse at what Eckhart Tolle, Alan Watts and all the other spiritual teachers I had listened to over the years were pointing to all along.

Chapter 20

The Power of Mentors

"Divide up your life. Spend 33% of your time around people lower than you, you can mentor them. Spend 33% of your time with people that are on your level - your friends and peers. Spend 33% of your time with people that are 10/20 years ahead of you. Those are your mentors." - Tai Lopez (Law of 33%)

Seek Help from Other People

I used to have a lone wolf mentality. After and perhaps prior to my experience with psychosis, I deeply mistrusted people. I thought to hell with everyone else I will figure this out myself.

This helped me to realise that I could be autonomous and that the most important thing is that I keep my word to myself. But in the words of the poet John Dunne - *"no man is an island, entire of itself"*.

I first became aware of the power of mentorship in 2015. Since then I have purchased books and hired 1 to 1 in-person mentors. These mentors and books have educated me on topics ranging from computer programming and linguistics to principles of the mind.

In my mid to late 20's I made the decision that the best investment would be to invest in my mind.

I had two primary reasons for doing this. The first was that I had experienced first-hand the immense psychological damage that can come from not understanding oneself.

The second reason was that I kept hearing some of the smartest and wealthiest people in the world say that investing in yourself is the most important thing anyone could do.

Delayed Gratification

I decided to commit to making this decision and play the long game. The most difficult part about investing in yourself is that you don't necessarily see where all your hard-earned money is going.

It isn't like purchasing a car or a house. With a car or a house, you can tangibly see your progress in life and you receive external validation from the people around you that you have made the right choice.

Over the years I have easily invested the price of a down payment on a fancy house in courses and 1 to 1 mentorship. Although this hasn't immediately brought me much in terms of material wealth or external validation, it has helped me to develop my skills and bring me a deeper understanding of my mind.

Up until my early 20's, I was deeply confused and internally conflicted without being aware of it. I don't think I was even looking for a deeper meaning and purpose to my life because I thought there was none.

I was predominantly living by someone else's rules whether it was religion, education or politics, I did my best to make sense of and internalize these rules in order to live a 'good' life. Living my life in this way only took me further away from my real voice and connecting with my own personal truths.

You're here to learn and grow

I didn't know there was a clear difference between religious dogma and the spiritual lessons underpinning every world religion.

I didn't know that the education system hadn't it all figured out. I didn't know that focusing on politics would lead me to take a back seat to my life and feeling like someone was going to come and save me when I messed up.

Investing time, energy and money in myself was my way of taking on more personal responsibility and taking my power back. It helped me to focus and prioritise what I wanted from my life and set priorities and boundaries.

I was always really bad at setting personal boundaries with other people. Again, I was trying to live by some fictious idea of a 'good' person and I ended up becoming a doormat to the wrong people far too many times.

I forgot the most important step when it comes to personal boundaries - learn to love and accept yourself first. Without this you might as well be attempting to bend the law of gravity to your will.

As I began to see that the rules, I had bought into weren't being enforced upon me it gave me some freedom of mind and hope. It often takes a serious amount of psychological pain to see through your own stories and self-limitations, psychosis started me on that path.

The Caveat to Keep in Mind

The right mentor can help you accelerate your growth. It's like they have a bird's eye view on your life and can spot the pit you have been stuck in for the past 7 years. Most likely because they were stuck in that pit for a long time themselves.

I have, however, come to realise that there is one important caveat to keep in mind if you make the decision to seek help from a mentor and that is to always follow your own path.

Do what works for You

When you respect someone and think they have a lot of knowledge it's very easy to buy into everything they tell you.

If you find the right mentor then they aren't telling you things to steer you wrong intentionally, they are just telling you what has worked for them and how they see the world.

Not everything that has worked for them will work for you. I wish I had learned this lesson earlier.

You both started from different places, with different life experiences and you could be heading in completely different directions so there will inevitably be differences between you.

Pay attention when something doesn't feel aligned for you and give weight to your own inner knowing.

Chapter 21

Beware of Group Think

"If everyone is thinking alike then somebody isn't thinking." - George S. Patton

What feels Personal is Universal

Being around like minded groups of people was vitally important for me. It helped me to take what had happened in my life less personally. It helped me to see I was more similar to other people then I had ever imagined. It helped me to realise that sharing my story could also help others.

When I started to see that my own personal problems were not unique to me I no longer felt different and weird for having them. I felt less isolated from other people and more connected. I had previously believed that most people had their shit together and so I had unrealistic expectations of myself.

Looking back I can see that the source of my problems was a lack of understanding. It wasn't that I was broken or weird or anything like that. I just didn't understand how to resolve the problems I was faced with.

I didn't know how to look at the world in a different way, in a way where I realised it was OK to be me and to create my own path in life.

Can't live with them, can't live without them

I was really curious in my 20's. I was open to learning about all sorts of things. The main areas of my focus were linguistics, computer programming, and human psychology. As a

151

result, I found myself among many different groups of people.

Although the people were often very different with very different ways of seeing the world, I noticed there was also a common thread to each group that wasn't entirely positive. In almost every group of people, I noticed an 'us v's them' mentality emerge somewhere.

It seems to be the nature of groups. I'm not sure how you could go about creating a group without positioning it in relation to some other group either consciously or unconsciously.

I have often seen this mentality, both in myself and in other people, fuel fears of being excluded from the group and a judgmental attitude towards those outside of the group. These judgements are usually wrapped around a great deal of misassumptions.

Group Blindspots

In my experience, groupthink and herd mentality are very real and dangerous phenomena. No matter what group I have found myself in there are almost always unspoken rules of how to act, behave and see the world.

To an extent this is helpful. It allows you to know the type of people you are around and whether you have shared interests and values.

However, I often see it become toxic when I feel like I need to filter my thoughts and words in order to fit in with the group.

This leaves me open to taking on the odd belief that isn't mine. In the moment it seems almost insignificant but over time unquestioned beliefs become your new limitations.

Even though what you do is a hundred times more important than what you will ever say when it comes to groups the fear of exclusion from the group seems to override this most basic of truths.

What does a happy life look like to me?

One of the questions that has helped me to stick to my own path in the most difficult moments has been *what does a happy life look like to me?*

This allows me to focus on my own life and to stay in my own lane. It allows me to ignore what other people are thinking and doing. At the end of the day, what is it all for if you can't say that you are happy to be alive?

Choose Uncomfortable

When I first came up with the name 'The Happy Mindset', I had no idea what I was trying to create.

I knew it had something to do with understanding the world beyond a purely surface level, harnessing the power of adversity and connecting to my own personal truths.

I didn't know what it would end up being beyond a simple blog where I expressed my thoughts about the world.

The name itself made me feel uncomfortable for a long time, which is probably why I chose it. This discomfort came from the thought of the many judgements I would inevitably face from what other people thought The Happy Mindset was all about.

Fear of the unknown is perhaps the greatest fear we face as human beings and I could clearly see this from my strong urge to need to know exactly what I was doing before I allowed myself to do it.

The idea of creating the podcast was in my head for a good year before I did it and writing this book has been in the back of my mind ever since I had my experience with psychosis.

Of course, sometimes there is a gestation period between thought and form. If I had tried to write this book a few months or even a few years after my experience I'm sure it would have been a complete car crash. Although I also know that if I was willing to learn from it it would have turned out alright in the end.

Speaking with the benefit of hindsight the moment it's right for you to begin is the point where you know you have just enough skill and understanding to get started and all you're being blocked by is your crippling fear.

As I am here writing this book for you you have proof that the crippling fear will never actually kill you although I can tell you that it always fells like it will.

People and opinions come and go

Over the years I have hired coaches who have supported what I do and took an interest in it, only for their interest to fade.

I have had friends who initially supported what I was doing only for some of them to do a complete 180 and become irritated by me and what I was doing. I have also hired a coach who said the name 'The Happy Mindset' is too broad and nobody cares about mindset anyway.

The point is that nobody is coming to save you and nobody is coming to do the work for you. The opinions I have received over the years are just that, opinions.

At the end of the day, you're the one who has to live with your own decisions and the nagging voice in the back of your head that will inevitably say *I told you to listen to me.*

If you want to make real and lasting change in your life then make a commitment to listen to and face yourself more and more each day.

Chapter 22

Ask Better Questions

"The definition of insanity is doing the same thing over and over again but expecting different results." - Albert Einstein

Mindless Repetition

No matter how naturally talented you are you always begin at a worse skill level than where you are now.

Michael Jordan, one of the greatest basketball players of all time was once cut from his high school basketball team. There are countless other stories where people who went on to do great things started life as a 'nobody' with no real undeniable talent or skill.

I discovered the power of repetition through language learning. I noticed that the more I repeated the process of learning new words the better I got at word retention.

Hardly a mind-blowing realisation but how many people do you know who tend to overlook consistently doing the simple things when it comes to tackling a complex topic?

Change the input to change the output

Repetition, however, has an upper limit. Not a lot of thought and brain power goes into repeating something.

You are simply handed a bunch of instructions and you repeat them until you become more efficient at the process. Repetition certainly has its place but you are not a robot, you are a human being.

As a human being living in a dynamic world when you keep repeating the same thing over and over again, you will eventually hit a wall.

The beauty of living in a dynamic world is that your results will change once you start changing your actions and behaviours. You can alter the input affecting your actions and behaviours whenever you make a conscious choice to do so.

Change the Question, Change your Life

The best way I know of really changing your actions and behaviours is to fundamentally alter the questions you take seriously.

By adjusting your questions from real world feedback, you are shifting from repetition to deliberate practice.

For a long time, I had an awareness of the importance of the questions I was asking myself but I had overlooked the importance of taking them seriously. I thought it was a nice to have and I was very much thinking about how I asked myself questions on a surface level.

I didn't really believe that questions could alter and change my reality in a profound and meaningful way so I didn't take them all that seriously.

Maybe this mental block came from my relationship with the word serious. I can remember been given an 'I'm entitled to be grumpy' badge as a child, it was the first time I was aware that other people perceived me in this light.

Like most things in life when I talk about taking your questions seriously there is a nuance to it. I don't mean coming from a place of force, insecurity and seeing other people as the enemy.

I mean really recognizing the true power of your questions to alter what you focus on and in turn shift your perception of the world around you.

Focus on the Process

"If it were easy everyone would do it."

- Muhammad Ali

Anything worthwhile isn't easy to achieve. Setting out to achieve something you haven't been able to do before requires growth on both a skills and an emotional level. If it didn't you would already be able to have your heart's desire.

Focusing on the process has allowed me to persevere in times where I felt like I was lost and making little to no progress. Over the years I have tried my hand at translating, coaching, freelancing, teaching and entrepreneurship with varying degrees of success and satisfaction.

Sometimes I would become disheartened and compare myself to some of my peers going through the 'normal' phases of life.

Sticking to one career path, buying a car, going on holidays, getting married and purchasing a house and think *what the hell am I doing with my life?, am I throwing my future away?*

In these moments it has been process based questions that have helped me to have faith and keep to my own path. Comparison is the thief of joy after all.

Here are some helpful questions to keep in mind:

- What am I learning here?

- Who am I becoming?

- Do I like the person I am becoming?

Winning at Life can be Simple

If you actually like who you are right now then, regardless of what your current circumstances look like, you are winning at life.

If you are not happy with the person you are then it isn't all bad news either. The truth of the matter is that your personality can change and adapt if you are willing to honestly ask yourself a different set of questions.

Simple question - profound implications

A fundamental question I realised I have been living with for many years is *how do I prove myself to others?* With this question in the back of my mind life feels like an endless interrogation.

I fear I will be found out in some way. I feel like I have to present a certain image to the world. This simple question makes it very difficult for me to be me, imperfections and all.

When I started to notice that this experience of life was coming from a question that was creating a perception and not from life itself, I saw that in these moments I need to take a pause, regain my bearings and change the question.

Instead of running around like a headless chicken forever trying to manage how the world perceives me I can now acknowledge the root cause and look in the direction of where the real work begins.

CHAPTER 23

THE POWER OF VULNERABILITY

"Because true belonging only happens when we present our authentic, imperfect selves to the world, our sense of belonging can never be greater than our level of self-acceptance."

- Brené Brown

Self-Acceptance

To be honest I am sometimes irritated by other people and think they are full of shit. I am sometimes irritated by myself and think I am full of shit. So, the initial thought of opening up to myself and to other people almost made me want to vomit.

It was completely foreign territory and I had no idea what to expect from it or of what purpose it served. I knew there was a big possibility of embarrassment. From being willing to be vulnerable I have come to see that it all hinges around self-acceptance.

When you open up about something you have kept secret for a long time there is no guarantee that the other person will react in the way you want them to.

Even if they do you are still held captive to the condition that they will continue to accept you as you are. But the other person's reaction is about them, not you, you can't control them, which brings us right back to self-acceptance.

Here are some questions that will help you determine when it is the right time for you to open up:

- Do I need to be accepted or validated from someone other than myself?

163

- Will any good come from me sharing my story?

You choose the chapters you show

Another distinction that I would like to make is that you don't have to be an open book to everyone. For a long time, I have struggled with this concept.

At one stage I thought the best way to get through life was to be as open and honest as I could be with everyone I met, but I was wrong.

People are very different and have very different ways of looking at the world. Unfortunately, there are people who will happily manipulate you for their own benefit.

I was way too honest with people I should have never trusted. I was too busy looking for acceptance from everyone and anyone to notice this. Over time as I have learned to accept myself more I have been able to pay better attention to the company I keep.

Sharing my Darkest Story

The most vulnerable thing I have ever done is to share the story of my experience with psychosis on my podcast and with you in this book. This story has represented a very dark time in my past and it was difficult to revisit it again even after all these years.

But revisiting this experience has helped me to heal and gain clarity, perspective and a sense of closure from it.

The Power of Surrender

Although how I navigated my experience has made me more resilient and helped me to understand the impact of societal stigma until I was able to fully acknowledge what had happened it hung over me in the back of my mind. I hadn't fully integrated it and I wasn't able to accept myself and fully move on.

Going through something very traumatic and on top of that living with shame and embarrassment for years after is no way for anyone to live.

After spending my 20's learning about the mind, the brain and the power of language I no longer wanted to feel this shame and embarrassment. I decided to close this chapter of my life and share my lessons to help you on your path.

Owning the Story

The scariest thing about sharing in public something you have kept secret is the unknown. Once it is out there it is out there.

My biggest fear was that I wouldn't be able to snap out of the traumatised mindset that I was caught up in when I thought about my experience with psychosis.

I didn't want to feel sorry for myself and for other people to look at me differently and feel sorry for me either. My mission is to help people perceive their traumas as opportunities for growth and embody a more empowering way of being in the world.

Sharing my own trauma while feeling like a victim was the last thing I wanted my life and my work to be about.

The first few times I shared my story on other podcasts was terrifying. Before the interviews, my mind would start racing at a hundred miles an hour.

The biggest thing that scared me was that once it was out it was out there was no turning back. The other thing that scared me was the thought that maybe all this stress and anxiety might trigger me into a state of psychosis again and I really didn't want to go back there.

Uncomfortable becomes Comfortable

What actually ended up happening was after some uncomfortable months of sharing, my mind started to adapt and I gradually overcame my fear of the story and what people think of me because of it.

It has been a longer process than I had expected. It hasn't been as simple as share my story once and I can move on. Focusing on the process and incremental progress is what has helped me muddle through in my own imperfect way.

All throughout my 20's I was extremely tentative to tell a close friend or a family member about my story. Now I can share this story with you in a book in a way that provides clarity and perspective around the lessons this trauma gifted me with. This is the good in my life that has come from sharing my story.

During this entire process, I have learned to accept myself more. I now realise that because I went through all that existential angst and psychological turmoil up until my early 20's I have gone on to lead a life that feels much more aligned with the real me.

Chapter 24

A Purpose Driven Life

"People take different roads seeking fulfillment and happiness, just because they're not on your road doesn't mean they have gotten lost."

- Dalai Lama

An Empty Feeling Inside

I guess I found my way to a sense of happiness and fulfillment by living in a state of discontentment and unhappiness first.

Prior to my 20's I didn't have a sense of purpose or direction in my life. I didn't have a deeper sense of why.

I just perceived myself on a purely surface and superficial level as a boy who would grow into a man, have a career, a house and hopefully, one day start a family. Anything beyond this seemed like wishful thinking and a pointless fantasy to me.

While intellectually it was easy for me to live in this way, I never had to ask myself the bigger existential questions like *what is the point of all this?* or *who am I really?*, it also left me with an empty feeling inside.

I didn't see life as an adventure or a puzzle to solve and I wasn't curious about who I was or the nature of the universe I lived in.

My outlook on life prior to having a mission, a purpose and a sense of direction would have been summed up nicely by Earl Nightengale when he said:

"Most people tiptoe their way through life, hoping they make it safely to death."

Once you are looking in the right direction, it's important to know that your mission and sense of purpose will change as you evolve as a person, so go with the flow of life and see where it takes you.

Create a Vision

Although I didn't know it back then, I accepted my first mission at 22 in the form of my experience with psychosis.

From that day onwards it was my mission to prove to myself that no matter what happens in my life I always have the power within to dig deeper and choose to live a happy and fulfilling life.

I started coming around to the idea of working on my vision around the time I turned 30. When I started to really think about it *how was I ever supposed to get anywhere in my life if I didn't have a vision to pull me forward? How would I know if I ever reached my destination? Maybe I have already hit many milestones but I haven't known what they were?*

These types of questions helped to knock me out of my overthinking trance when it came to working on a vision for my life. It was beginning to make logical sense to me. Once it started to make sense, I started to allow myself to start writing out a vision for my life.

If you want a simple exercise to see if you have any types of limiting beliefs then sit down with a pen and paper and write out a vision for your life. Break your vision into health, wealth, relationships, self-mastery and happiness. Spend some time writing out the best vision possible for your life.

Think and Dream Bigger

Doing these exercises made me feel very uncomfortable. There is still resistance there today when I take the time to do it.

Even something as simple as writing this book was included in my vision. It wasn't as specific as *I will write a book about what I learned in my 20's to help the reader transform their adversity into their personal power* but simply writing down *I will be a published author* felt difficult to write. It felt grandiose to me and like I shouldn't be so bold or aim so high in life.

It was even more difficult to write *I will be a best-selling author*. I don't know why it's so difficult, but it probably ties in somewhere with the old mantra about low expectations that I had unconsciously internalised as a teenager.

You are not your goals

Whenever I write down big goals it still initially feels like if I want to commit to this then I am putting my self-worth on the line.

171

The truth is that I'm not. Sure, I will be disappointed if I don't create some of the things I want to see come into fruition but the type of person I become in the process is the most important thing simply because this is the one and only thing that I ever really have a say in.

When I look at it this way then what is the point in aiming low in life when it takes the same amount of energy to aim high?

CHAPTER 25

DISCOVER WHAT YOU VALUE

"When the voice and vision on the inside is more profound, and more clear and loud than all opinions on the outside, you've begun to master your life." - Dr. John F. Demartini.

What do you value?

I used to think about values in a moralistic way. I didn't know any better because I had no other reference point to think about values other than through a religious and moralistic lens. I don't remember learning what values are and why they are important in school.

I thought that being a man of value was about looking out for others and putting their needs first. When I would fall short of these notions then I felt like there was something wrong with me or I wasn't doing enough to live up to these standards.

My vague notions of morals and values largely turned out to be toxic and confusing. I was rarely paying attention to what I valued and when I did, I was looking at them the wrong way around.

You can't give what you don't have and if you don't take the time to take care of yourself first then you won't be capable of really taking care of anyone else.

From reading books such as *The Values Factor* by Dr John Demartini and from being around life coaches over the past few years I have come to see the importance of being aware of what you value the most in your life.

You're already living by a set of values

Instead of thinking of values as defining who I am as a person I began to think of them as things that helped me clarify what I want in my life.

Values aren't optional. You're already living by a set of values whether you know it or not. When I was unaware of my values, I was often living by values that didn't serve me.

One such value was the need for acceptance which had me spending my time doing things I didn't care about or really enjoy. Things like going to the pub every weekend and drinking myself silly.

At first, I found this really difficult as I sat with a pen and paper writing out what I value. I was drawing a complete blank the first few times. Questions that would emerge were of the variety of *what is the point of this?, what is a value?*

When I managed to write down some of my values, I could see the internal conflicts emerge between what I actually valued and what I thought I should value.

Unconscious Values

The biggest thing that emerged for me, that had remained largely unconscious, was the value I had placed on being right. When operating from this value system I didn't really see making mistakes as part of learning.

I might have been able to verbalise the importance of making mistakes but my value system wasn't fully aligned with my words.

In my value system mistakes were still something to be ashamed of and avoided at all costs and no amount of words would shift this until I acknowledged that being right was something I valued.

The truth will set you free

Once I had consciously admitted this to myself, I was able to become more intentional about shifting my value system to internalize the value of continuous learning, a value that has always served me well.

By consciously choosing this as a value I am able to remind myself of what I truly value when I make mistakes and start to get lost in a haze of self-doubt and self-criticism.

At Sea without a Rudder

Take a minute right now and look around the room you are in. Look at the items you surround yourself with. What are they?

These are the things that you value the most at this point in your life. This is such a simple exercise but one that I was not aware of until it was pointed out to me.

Until I started to get clear on what I truly valued most in life I was like a ship at sea without a rudder. A ship being bounced around by what other people valued and what I thought I should value.

It might be difficult to begin with but understanding what you truly value will help you to understand when you feel like a victim and what choice you actually have in the matter. It's a small price to pay for increased mental freedom and a better quality of life.

Chapter 26

Full Circle

"My advice if someone wrote something and hurt your feelings is to stand on a street corner and watch all the people walk by. I bet you none of those people are thinking about you."

- Jeff Bezos.

Living Life Below the Head

When I first got interested in the mind and the brain, I was purely looking at it from an intellectual point of view.

Self-awareness 101 wasn't exactly taught in school and so all throughout my formative and teenage years, I struggled with what was really going on for me on an emotional level.

I didn't think it was important to understand my emotions as there was no emphasis on building self-awareness and emotional intelligence at school.

Emotional intelligence simply wasn't seen as an important factor behind long-term success and happiness when I went to school. I don't think emotional intelligence was even a term people referenced back then.

A disconnected life

When I decided to make it my mission to learn about my mind and my brain for the first few years, I wasn't willing to venture much further below the head.

This wasn't even a conscious decision on my part, my head had become so disconnected from my body that I didn't even know I was living like this.

To some extent it helped. Learning about flight or fight mode, the amygdala, the RAS area of the brain and neural pathways all helped me to understand the human body and human potential on a level I never quite understood before.

A new language isn't just a bunch of words

However, there came a point when I realised that the answer wasn't going to come from adding more information into my brain.

There is a certain level of research and due diligence you need to do to sufficiently educate yourself about a topic but there comes a stage where you reach a tipping point and the law of diminishing returns starts to quickly kick in.

It was like the day I realised that I wouldn't become fluent in French by learning all the French words.

For me, that day came when I realised that I was still feeling the same old feelings about myself and I had no idea why.

The first major step I took towards understanding my emotions better came from the online courses I took at Mind Valley. The next major steps in this direction came from some hypnotherapy sessions, body and energy work sessions and training to become a life coach.

These experiences led me to paying more attention to my emotions and understanding the many sophisticated tricks my mind plays on me to stop me from feeling certain emotions.

Simplicity amid Complexity

Understanding my emotions has been the simplest and yet the most complex thing I have ever set about doing.

Over the last few years, I have frequently lost touch with being human as I unwittingly attempted to avoid certain emotions by trying to understand them better on an intellectual level.

It sometimes feels to me that if I give my mind a general objective then it will constantly mull it over in the background, sort of like the anti-virus on your computer, you only ever know it is running when a problem appears or it's hogging all the resources.

I have learned time and time again that emotional integration is the answer and not personal judgement created in the mind.

Thankfully there is a positive to this unconscious behaviour. Great inventors such as Thomas Edison have been known to use this aspect of the human mind to their advantage by handing over questions to their subconscious mind to work on throughout the night.

Willingness to Learn + Action

Taking action and feeling the uncomfortable emotions that come from the action has allowed me to understand more about myself than any book or mentor has taught me.

It is when combining a willingness to learn with action that I don't feel so stuck in my life. They are like two sides of the same coin.

When I just take action and ignore the real questions and assumptions behind what I think I want then I eventually get stuck.

When the only learning I do is in an echo chamber of a classroom or behind a computer screen and I am missing real-world feedback then I also get stuck. It has been through a combination of the two that the whole comes together for me.

I had spent the first half of my 20's focused on building better habits and asking better questions. I had spent most of the second half exploring principles of the mind and understanding my emotions better.

As I approached my 30th birthday I realised that it was time to start unifying the two and become my own man with my own voice.

CHAPTER 27

USE YOUR OWN WORDS

"When nobody else celebrates you, learn to celebrate yourself. When nobody else compliments you, then compliment yourself. It's not up to other people to keep you encouraged. It's up to you. Encouragement should come from the inside." - Jay Shetty

A Never-Ending Dance

At some point in your journey, you will realise that there is no one 'right' answer to anything in your life.

Everybody is learning their own lessons on their own individual journeys. There is only what works for you to help you make progress in your own life.

This isn't to say that you can't give or receive advice. Open your mind and experiment until you find what works for you at each step of the way. Remain conscious to when you find yourself slipping into a dogmatic way of thinking, it never feels good.

Don't Forget Your Heart

I am gradually finding my most helpful answers by learning to use both my brain and my heart. My brain is practical and pragmatic and it keeps me safe. It knows my tolerance to risk and I respect and honour that.

However, it will never allow me to know who I am or what I am capable of. If I had simply listened to my brain when I went through psychosis, I don't know what my life would look like right now. That is where my heart and soul come in.

My soul knows it's unconquerable, it likes to be free and express who I really am but it's also like a wild stallion that I don't really understand.

I have to take the time to quiet my mind and listen to it because it knows what I truly want. I then can use my brain more wisely to experiment with ways to manifest my heart's desire in the real world.

From psychosis, I saw that a life lived using just my brain feels empty, confusing, disconnected and depressing. A life lead solely with my heart feels liberating but also chaotic and manic.

Learning to combine the two is where I have had a sense of progress, happiness and fulfillment in my life

Break free of Black and White Thinking

I have mentioned the archaic mind and black and white thinking quite a few times already in this book. You will go through many phases of black and white thinking.

This way of thinking comes natural to you and it requires very little thought and energy. It allows you to conceptualise and make sense of the world without being completely disoriented, lost and overwhelmed by the enormous amounts of information your brain receives every day.

When looking at life through this lens you will often think this thing over here is the answer and you will overlook or overemphasize other things based on a mixture of your opinion and other people's opinions. You will also misinterpret what other people say based on your own beliefs and your own life experiences.

Context and remaining adaptable are key ingredients and your ability to learn will far outweigh your ability to passively take in information or self-righteously hold on to beliefs that may actually be limiting you.

Become an alchemist

By keeping an open mind, you will come to realise that everything is white noise until you begin to synthesise and internalise the information for yourself.

Become your own alchemist creating your own gold. Don't just purchase someone else's indefinitely, that is if you want to become the master of your own destiny and not just a mere puppet.

When you start cultivating the capacity within you to create your own gold, you no longer have to worry about the supply from elsewhere.

The Dangers of Language Filtering

I was learning Spanish and Italian when I had my experience with psychosis at 22. In that year I experienced immense possibility and immense pain and darkness all at once. It was overwhelming to say the least.

The dark side of my experience gave me the motivation to educate myself on things that actually mattered to me.

For so many years my mind had associated education with regurgitation and measuring up to someone else's predefined set of standards that I had almost completely lost my love of learning.

Simple shifts

From this simple shift in my relationship with learning, I learned more about myself over the following years than I ever thought possible. The bright side gave me the understanding that no obstacle is too big and anything really is possible if you put your mind to it.

Over the years I have been to many different seminars, events, and retreats. I have taken countless courses and read hundreds of books across numerous different disciplines.

Looking back on all the moments of chaos and clarity and the ups and downs the one piece of advice I would give to you would be to always use your own words and look to connect with your real voice.

The Dark Side of Censorship

As I look back on my teenage and early adult years, I can see that the path to getting lost in conformity began with language filtering.

If a certain way of looking at the world didn't seem to be acceptable then I began to gradually erase it from my vocabulary.

Before I started consciously and unconsciously filtering my language, I didn't understand the importance of context or that groups of people can have very different sets of beliefs.

I didn't realise it was OK to think differently. I also didn't understand the freedom of choice I had when it came to where I placed my attention.

Had I known all these things maybe my choices would have been different. I think the momentum of filtering my language was a key reason as to why I was blinded from learning about all these subtle nuances in human behaviour from an earlier age.

Your problems don't exist 'out there'

If I were to describe my experience with psychosis as a specific feeling then it would be the feeling of not being heard.

You know the feeling you get when you are playing charades with a particularly bad partner? That overwhelming feeling of sheer frustration when it finally dawns on you that no matter what you do, they will never get it.

That was what psychosis felt like for me. Initially, I thought that I needed to be understood by the world. A daunting task and one that I didn't truly believe was possible or worth my time and effort.

Nevertheless, this is where my story began. I might not have needed to convince the world but in the worst moments imaginable I needed to find a way to help other people comprehend what was happening inside my head so that I could receive the right help.

It took a misdiagnosis of depression but I eventually received the correct medication that helped to bring the chemicals in my brain back into order. It was then that my real life's work began.

Listen to Yourself

For the first few years, I was looking the wrong way around. I was looking at the world and trying to figure it out. I thought all the answers would come from understanding other people and the world around me. I thought it would take a long time but it would be worth the endeavor.

At some point on my journey, I realised I had the binoculars on the wrong way around. I didn't need to understand the world and it didn't need to understand me. What I needed to do all along was to take the time to listen to and understand myself.

Why I Love Language

Be it a human language or a computer programming language my love of language is at the heart of everything I do. I am drawn to languages for 3 specific reasons.

The first is that it occupies my analytical mind on something concrete and tangible. My analytical mind wasn't built to understand itself or the known universe. When it attempts to do so it slowly begins to drive me nuts. My experience with psychosis has woken me up to the immense destruction a human mind out of control can do.

The second is that language helps me to grow and develop into a better person. Language presents me with the words that I am emotionally triggered by so that I can take a closer look at what is really going on for me.

'Swat', 'foreigner', 'psychotic' are all words that have been presented to me over the years. After taking a closer look at my own psychology these words no longer leave the same bad taste in my mouth that they once did.

The words themselves are never the real issue, they only serve as a pointer to where we have the opportunity to begin the real work.

The third is that learning a new foreign language or a computer programming language isn't easy. It requires focus, discipline and the ability to make sense of and conceptualise a communication tool. Focusing my mind in this way has helped me to build a level of resilience and persistence I might not otherwise have built.

Unlock Your Unique Energy

Ultimately, it's the energy and intention behind your words that matters more than the words themselves.

It took me almost a decade to realise this one. This energy is what people really pay attention to and connect with. It will take time to connect with your unique energy and get a feel for it.

Don't rush it, don't judge yourself for not being as powerful as the people you tend to compare yourself to.

It was meant to take time. In the long run you will be glad you allowed your real self the time and space necessary to evolve instead of caving in to the quick fix of pretending to be someone more 'acceptable'.

Parting Words

Shit happens in life and it will often times feel undeserved and unfair. It's easy to live feeling like a victim to circumstance but it comes at the cost of a hard life psychologically. Believe me, I have been there and bought the t-shirt.

I thought I had to constantly keep up to date with the news to stay informed even though it depressed me and negatively distorted my perception of the world.

I thought it wasn't OK to be vulnerable. I thought it wasn't OK to be interested in things

191

other people didn't understand or thought were weird. I thought I had to enjoy getting drunk at the weekend to fit in with my peers and be sociable.

I had all these misperceptions and assumptions that limited and misguided me. Sure, there are people who will think you are weird and won't agree with your opinions but would you rather live like a shadow of yourself or live like your real self?

So there you have it, these were some of the unexpected lessons I learned in my 20's because of the experience I had with psychosis.

It was a rollercoaster ride between order and chaos but it was also a deeply rewarding experience to eventually come out the other side stronger than you entered.

The final insight I will leave you with is this – your life will ultimately be what you make of it, just make sure that at the end of the day you can say you gave it your best and you lead your own life.

Fin

APPENDIX

How are habits formed: Modelling habit formation in the real world by Phillippa Lally, Cornelia H.M van Jaarsveld, Henry W. W. Potts, Jane Wardle

https://onlinelibrary.wiley.com/doi/abs/10.1002/ejsp.674

25 Cognitive Biases that Ruin Your Life, Explained by Allen Cheng

https://www.allencheng.com/25-cognitive-biases-charlie-munger/

The first 20 hours – how to learn anything by Josh Kaufman - TedxCSU

https://www.youtube.com/watch?v=5MgBikgcWnY

Positive Psychology: An Introduction by Martin E. P. Seligman

https://www.researchgate.net/publication/11946304_Positive_Psychology_An_Introduction

Tai's Top Book Recommendations

https://www.tailopez.com/books

What is an Ambivert? Take the Quiz to See if you're an Introvert, Extrovert or Ambivert

https://www.scienceofpeople.com/ambivert

Printed in Great Britain
by Amazon